THE NEW RUSSIA

DATE DUE

12-11-01			

THE NEW RUSSIA

DISCOVERING our HERITAGE

By John Gillies

 **DILLON PRESS**
New York

Maxwell Macmillan Canada
Toronto

Maxwell Macmillan International
New York Oxford Singapore Sydney

Photo Credits

Cover by: George H. Cummings

John Gillies, pages 10, 120; George H. Cummings, pages 14, 16-17, 19, 56-57, 93; The Bettmann Archive, pages 28, 31, 81, 103; Linda Evans, pages 38, 41, 66, 97, 100, 118; The Associated Press, page 48; The Stock Market, pages 54, 78; The Conner Center, page 59; The Limited Edition, page 68; Dave Bartruff, page 70, 82, 87, 90; Alaska Division of Tourism, page 108; Wide World Photos, page 115

Library of Congress Cataloging-in-Publication Data

Gillies, John, 1925-
    The New Russia / by John Gillies. — 1st ed.
      p. cm. — (Discovering our heritage)
    Includes bibliographical references and index.
    Summary: Provides a description of the Russian Federation, from a social and geographical perspective.
    ISBN 0-87518-481-2
    1. Russia (Federation)—Juvenile literature. [1. Russia (Federation)] I. Title. II. Series.
DR67.7.G55 1994
947.086—dc20   93-25380

Printed on recycled paper

Dillon Press   Maxwell Macmillan Canada, Inc.
Macmillan Publishing Company   1200 Eglinton Avenue East
866 Third Avenue   Suite 200
New York, NY 10022   Don Mills, Ontario M3C 3N1

Macmillan Publishing Company is part of the Maxwell Communication Group of Companies.

First edition

10 9 8 7 6 5 4 3 2 1

Contents

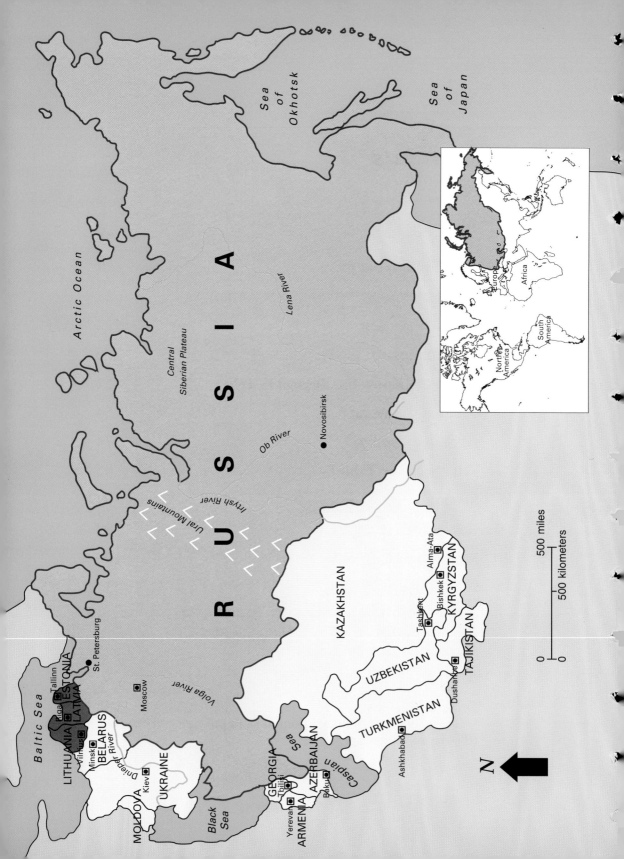

Fast Facts about Russia

Official Name: Russian Federation

Capital: Moscow

Location: Russia covers nearly one-half of Europe and one-third of Asia. To its north is the Arctic Ocean; to the north-west, Norway, Finland, Latvia, and Estonia; to the west, Belarus (formerly Byelorussia) and Ukraine; to the south (in Europe), the Black Sea, Georgia, Azerbaijan, Kazakhstan, and the Caspian Sea; to the south (in Asia), Mongolia, China, and North Korea; its eastern border is the Sea of Japan, the Pacific Ocean, the Bering Sea, and the Sea of Okhotsk. The western region of Kaliningrad (former East Prussia) touches Lithuania, Poland, and the Baltic Sea.

Area: 6,592,692 square miles (17,075,072 square kilometers). From east to west, its greatest distance is 6,800 miles (10,968 kilometers), and from north to south it is 3,200 miles (5,162 kilometers).

Elevation: *Highest*—Mount Elbrus (Caucasus range), 18,481 feet (5,633 meters) above sea level. *Lowest*—Karagiye Depression (or Batyr Sink), 433 feet (132 meters) below sea level. It is in Kazakhstan.

Population: Estimated population for 1992, 149,300,000. *Distribution*—74 percent of the people live in or near cities, 26 percent in rural areas. *Density*—23.3 persons per square mile (9 persons per square kilometer). Population over age 65: 10 percent; under age 15, 23 percent.

Form of Government: Constitutional Republic. Its legislature, the Congress of People's Deputies (1,033 elected members), meets only occasionally. A Parliament (252 members), still called the Supreme Soviet, meets regularly to pass laws; its members are members of the Congress. When and if a new constitution is adopted, a bicameral congress is planned, similar to the U.S. Senate and House of Representatives. A Constitutional Court, similar to the U.S. Supreme Court, now decides whether present laws are constitutional. The presiding officer of the Congress and Parliament is the prime minister. The president, who selects the cabinet, is elected by the people. Russia is a member of the Commonwealth of Independent States (CIS), which is made up of 10 of the 15 republics of the former Soviet Union; Russia is also a member of the International Monetary Fund (IMF) and the United Nations (UN).

Some Important Products: *Agriculture*—Barley, corn, cotton, oats, potatoes; beef cattle, dairy cattle, sheep. *Industry*—chemicals, electrical products, iron and steel, lumber, bauxite, coal, copper, iron ore, petroleum, transportation equipment, machinery

Basic Unit of Money: Ruble

Major Language: Russian (82 percent of the population is Russian). There are 50 nationality groups within Russia, with 31 ethnic administrative areas. Other major languages: Ukrainian, Uzbek, Belorussian, Kazakh, and Tatar.

Major Religions: Russian Orthodox, 35 percent; Islam, 10 percent; Protestant, 4 percent; Roman Catholic, 1 percent; Jewish, 1 percent. (Percentages are estimated. The previous Soviet government officially discouraged religion.)

Flag: Horizontal tricolor; white on top, then blue and red.

Major Holidays: New Year's Day, January 1; Epiphany, January 6; May Day (Labor Day), May 1; Victory in Europe Day (end of World War II), May 9; Independence Day, June 8; Revolution Day, November 7; CIS Anniversary, December 8; Christmas, December 25.

Moscow's famous skyline: the "onion" domes of St. Basil's

1. The New Russia: Where and What It Is

The new Russia is very much *like* the old imperial Russia in size and culture, before it became part of the Soviet Union. The new Russia is very much *unlike* that old Russia, both in its form of government and its economy.

The country we once knew as the USSR (the Union of Soviet Socialist Republics) ceased to exist in 1991. For many years, and for many reasons, the USSR was considered an enemy and, later, a rival of the countries representing the "free world." Those were the times after World War II when people talked a lot about the cold war and the iron curtain, which were images of the harsh divisions between the East and the West.

Another symbol of that division was former East Germany's Berlin Wall. It was built in 1961 and although it was only 26½ miles (43 kilometers) long, it kept thousands of East Germans from seeking freedom in the West. The Berlin Wall was torn down in 1989 and shortly thereafter East and West Germany were reunited. With Germany's unification, the vast Soviet empire began to crumble. Communist governments were toppled in such Soviet satellite countries as Poland, Czechoslovakia, Hungary, Romania, and Bulgaria. Within the Soviet Union itself, individual republics began to break away. The political boundaries of central and Eastern Europe were reshaped.

From 1922 to 1991, Russia was part of the Union of Soviet Socialist Republics, sharing a hundred languages and the traditions of 14 other countries. During that period it was governed by the Communist party.

Now both the Soviet Union and the strength of the Communist party have faded away. Russia is once again sovereign and independent. Russia now belongs to a Commonwealth of Independent States (CIS), of which Russia is the major partner. Russia occupies three-fourths of the Commonwealth's territory, has one-half of its population, and supports 60 percent of its industry.

Once Russia had a king (called a czar). Later, as part of the USSR, it was ruled by dictators, although they were called by other names, such as "party chairmen" and "general secretaries." Today it has a president, a congress, and many political parties. Russia is striving to be a democracy.

A new era for Russia and the Russian people has begun.

Where It Is

Russia is part of both Europe and Asia, beginning at the Gulf of Finland in the west and ending at the Bering Sea in the east. There is no precise boundary between Europe and Asia, but in Russia it is generally accepted as the Ural Mountains and the Ural River, which flows into the Caspian Sea.

Russia's northern border is the Arctic Ocean. In the south, it touches the Black Sea and the Caspian Sea. Its neighbors in the east include Japan and Alaska (across the

Bering Sea); to the south, China, Mongolia, North Korea, and the Commonwealth states of Kazakhstan and Georgia; to its west, Ukraine, Belarus, Lithuania (bordering Kaliningrad), Latvia, Estonia, Finland, and Norway.

A tiny part of Russia touches the Baltic Sea and borders Lithuania and Poland. It is separated from greater Russia. This area is called Kaliningrad and was formerly known as East Prussia, which was then a part of Germany.

What It Is

When you think of Russia, you must think of the word *big*. Russia is a country of 150 million people. It occupies one-sixth of the world's land surface, which makes it the largest country on earth. When you travel from one end of the country to the other, from east to west (or west to east), you must change your watch 11 times; Russia has 11 time zones.

Several of its rivers are longer than the Mississippi. The Volga is the longest river in Europe and flows into the Caspian Sea. The Lena, in Siberia, flows northward into the Arctic Ocean. Other important rivers are the Dnieper, Don, Ob, Yenisey, and Amur. Many of these rivers have dams with hydroelectric power plants.

The deepest lake in the world is Lake Baikal in Siberia. More than a mile deep, it contains one-fifth of the entire world's supply of fresh water, although in recent years it has been polluted by industrial waste.

When you look at the width of Russia on a map, you

The statue of St. Vladimir above the Dnieper River

might think of a three-layer cake. In the south is the layer known as the steppe, which is derived from a Russian word meaning "lowland." It is similar to the North American prairie or South American pampa (grassland). These flat-lands begin in independent Ukraine and continue eastward into Asia and contain some of the richest soil in the world. In Asia the steppe becomes a desert.

The next layer is the taiga, a birch-and-pine forest that extends from Norway through Siberia to the Bering Sea for 6,000 miles (9,660 kilometers).

The top layer might be called the "icing on the cake." These frozen marshlands, or tundra, are found along the treeless Arctic coast. Except for moss and lichens, there is no vegetation. The subsoil is permanently frozen.

Russia's chief mountain ranges are the Caucasus, stretching from the Black Sea to the Caspian Sea; the Urals, going vertically for 1,300 miles (2,093 kilometers) south to north, dividing Europe and Asia; the Altays, which border Kazahkstan; and the Sayans, which separate Siberia from Mongolia.

Resources

Russia is rich in raw materials, such as timber, nickel, iron, bauxite, gold, diamonds, and furs. It is especially fortunate in energy. Russia produces 22 percent of the world's oil, 16 percent of its coal, and 40 percent of its natural gas. It has nine nuclear power plants, which generate electricity.

Russia is less fortunate in agriculture. Its rich soil ought to be able to produce all of the food it needs. However, droughts often result in reduced harvests. Farms are inefficient, and transportation is lacking. Russia inherited many agricultural problems from the former Soviet system. The country wants to do away with the large and inefficient government farms. It also wants to improve transportation so that food products get to the cities promptly.

The Commonwealth of Independent States

The former Soviet Union was made up of 15 republics. After the collapse of the USSR in 1991, 10 of those republics formed a Commonwealth of Independent States (CIS); one

Russia's Caucasus Mountains

of these is Russia, whose official name is the Russian Federation.

Commonwealth is understood to mean an association of self-governing states united by an agreement to do certain things together. The Commonwealth members decided they would use the same kind of money, have a single foreign affairs office, and cooperate in a single command of the armed forces. As self-governing (autonomous) states, each republic has its own legislature and its own flag.

Nine states have joined with Russia to form the new Commonwealth. They are Armenia, Belarus, Kazakhstan, Kyrgyzstan, Moldava, Tajikistan, Turkmenistan, Ukraine, and Uzbekistan.

Armenia has 3.5 million people and its borders touch Turkey and Iran. Its capital is Yerevan. From there, on a clear day you can see Mount Ararat, in Turkey, where Noah is supposed to have grounded his ark.

Belarus has 10.5 million people and touches Lithuania. Its capital is Minsk, where the first meeting of the Commonwealth was held.

Kazakhstan has 17 million people and is the second-largest state in land area in the CIS, after Russia. It borders China. Its chief resource is coal. Kazakhstan's capital is Alma-Ata.

Kyrgyzstan has 4.5 million people and also shares a border with China. Its capital is Bishkek.

Moldava has about 4 million people and touches Romania and Ukraine; Romanian is its primary language. Its capital is Kishinev.

Yerevan, Armenia, with Mount Ararat in the background

Tajikistan has 5.5 million people and shares borders with China and Afghanistan. The highest mountains in the Commonwealth are located in the Pamir range; ten are higher than 20,000 feet (6,100 meters). Its capital is Dushanbe.

Turkmenistan has nearly 4 million people and is the Commonwealth's southernmost country, touching both Afghanistan and Iran. Its capital is Ashkhabad.

Ukraine is the second-most-populous Commonwealth state after Russia, with 52 million people. Because of its rich soil, Ukraine is the agricultural "breadbasket" of the Commonwealth. It is also a major source of iron ore. Its capital is Kiev.

Uzbekistan has almost 20 million people. Its neighbors are Turkmenistan, Kazakhstan, and Tajikistan. It shares a border with Afghanistan. Its chief agricultural product is cotton. Its capital is Tashkent.

Former Soviet Republics That Are Not Part of the Commonwealth

Five former Soviet republics broke away from the Soviet Union and rejected membership in the new Commonwealth.

Azerbaijan has 7 million people and shares its border with Iran. Its territory is divided by Armenia, with which it has a dispute over the region called Nagorno-Karabakh. Azerbaijan's capital is Baku, on the Caspian Sea.

Georgia (also known as Gruziya) has 5.5 million people. Its coastline faces the Black Sea. A region called South Ossetia wants to secede and become part of Russia. Georgia's capital is Tbilisi. Georgia may join the Commonwealth.

Estonia has 1.6 million people and is the northernmost Baltic republic, located south of Finland. The Estonian language is similar to Finnish and Hungarian. Its capital is Tallinn.

Latvia has nearly 3 million people and is also located along the Baltic Sea, across from Sweden. Its capital is Riga.

Lithuania has nearly 4 million people. This Baltic republic shares borders with Belarus, Poland, and Russia

(Kaliningrad region). The Lithuanian and Latvian languages are similar. Lithuanian is the oldest language spoken in Europe. Lithuania's capital is Vilnius.

The Russian Federation

Russia has joined with 20 other entities to form the Russian Federation. Fifteen of these are called autonomous republics and each enjoys some form of self-government. Some are seeking independence, such as the Checheno-Ingush, Karelian, South Ossetian, and Tatar republics.

Five members of the Federation are called "autonomous regions." Most are small, with populations of less than 100,000. One of these is the Jewish ("Yevreysk") region, located in eastern Siberia, north of Manchuria.

2. How Russia Began

Before it had a name, the land now called Russia was a magnet, attracting wandering tribes. Some were hungry, looking for food. A few were greedy, looking for markets or conquests. Others were just adventurers, wanting to discover new territories. What attracted them was the steppe, that vast prairie without trees, without obstacles, that had the deepest, richest soil known to humans. Such land meant food and prosperity.

People already lived there, but we don't know who they were. Russia has been inhabited for at least 30 centuries, before people wrote history. We don't even know what language the people spoke. If they could write, no one has yet found any evidence of it. We only know that there was lots of shedding and mixing of blood before a new nation was born. The Slavs from the east became the dominant nationality.

The first invaders were the Scythians, who came from the south, perhaps from Persia (known today as Iran). The Scythians were expert horsemen and extremely cruel fighters. They drank the blood of the first person they killed in a battle. They scalped their victims.

The Scythians in turn were defeated by the Sarmatians, who were followed by other conquering tribes: the Goths from Germany, the Bulgars from the Balkans, the Huns from Asia, and the Avars from Turkey.

Another tribe lived in the north, in the forests, or the taiga. These were the northern Slavs, who built settlements and cities for protection. They, too, were often under attack—from the Khazars in the east and Mordvinians (or Finns) in the west. The Slavs won and lost battles, welcomed their conquerors, found a way to "get along," and survived.

The Slavs spoke a language that is the root of modern Russian, Polish, Czech, Bohemian, Belorussian, Serbian, Wendish, Bulgarian, and Ukrainian. These are called Slavic languages.

The dawn of written history about Russia begins with the 9th century A.D. It starts with a man called Rurik, who wasn't even a Russian. Rurik was a Viking, a leader of a band called the Varangians, who captured the Slavic fortified city of Novgorod in A.D. 862, collected taxes, and set up a government. Rurik ruled until 879.

The Vikings were Scandinavian warriors and sailors, and were the first world explorers. The Vikings were probably the first people to visit the North American continent, perhaps at the same time that others of their tribe were invading Russia. The Vikings, or Varangians, who occupied this area were called Rus or Rhos, and many believe this may be how the name *Russia* (or *Rossiya*, in Russian) came about. The Slavs accepted the Vikings and themselves became known as the Rus or Russians. For about the next 750 years, until 1598, all the kings of Russia claimed to be descendants of Rurik.

Novgorod, the city captured by Rurik, means "new city" in Russian. It was a trading center built by the Slavs in an area just south of what today is St. Petersburg. German and Scandinavian merchants came to Novgorod to barter their goods for furs and amber. Novgorod still exists and has been rebuilt to look like it did in those early days. In fact, it is often used as a movie set for historical motion pictures.

In the year 890, Prince Oleg moved his capital from Novgorod to Kiev, far to the south on the Dnieper River.

Rivers Are Highways

Before there were paved highways or railroads, the best way for people to travel was by river. Except for an occasional waterfall or rapids, rivers are mostly smooth, liquid highways. The Dnieper River was just such a river-highway in Russia. If you look at a map of Eastern Europe, you can trace its course. To the south of Kiev, it flows into the Black Sea. If you follow the northern shore of the Black Sea, you will find the mouth of the Danube River. You can sail the Danube past Vienna, Austria, into central Europe. If you continued on the Black Sea, avoiding the Danube, you would arrive at Istanbul, Turkey. Istanbul is the modern name for the ancient city of Constantinople.

Looking again at your map, return to Kiev. Sailing north from Kiev on the Dnieper, you come to the city of Smolensk. Travel farther, and you will cross a short stretch of land and come to another river called the Volkhov. It will take you back to that first capital city of Novgorod, and beyond it to Lake Ladoga to the Gulf of Finland. And again, sailing into the Baltic Sea, you will have found another gateway to Europe.

Kiev and Constantinople

Grand Prince Vladimir (who ruled from 980 to 1015) and his nobles sailed southward on the Dnieper River to the Black Sea. Their destination was Constantinople, named for the Roman emperor Constantine the Great. It had become a major commercial center, linking Europe with Asia.

The Slavs, or Rus, brought slaves or merchandise such as furs, grain, amber, and lumber they hoped to sell. The officials in Constantinople were suspicious of these strange "northerners." The Slavs were allowed to enter Constantinople through a single gate, and they had to check their weapons. They were instructed to sell their goods and slaves as quickly as possible and then return to their homeland.

The Slavs stayed long enough to be impressed with Constantinople's wealth and culture, as well as with its religion. One hundred years after Rurik's descendants had come to Kiev, Grand Prince Vladimir formally accepted Christianity, as expressed by the Eastern Orthodox church in Constantinople. In A.D. 988, Vladimir was baptized in the Dnieper River and ordered his subjects to be baptized with him. For many years, Kiev was the headquarters of the new Orthodox church, which for the next thousand years would serve as the official state church of Russia.

The Descendants of Genghis Khan

The Slavic tribes were attacked in 1220 by the Mongols. They came from Asia, through the Caucasus Mountains. The Mongols were called Tatars (sometimes misspelled "Tartars"). They were recruited and led by Batu, the grandson of the famous Genghis Khan, whose capital, Karakorum, was in China. The fearsome Tatars were called the Golden Horde, a name they got from their brightly colored tents, which reflected the sun.

The Mongols captured Kiev in 1242.

At the same time, the northern Slavic tribes fought invading Swedes and Germans. Their leader was Alexander Nevsky, who also fought the Mongols and was killed in a battle with them. The Mongol-Tatars were now clearly in command. They taxed the people and set up puppet kingdoms with Slavic princes who would obey them. No one dared to challenge the Tatars for two centuries.

Moscow Enters the Story

Meanwhile, the Slavic kingdom of Muscovy, in the northeast, grew stronger, even though it continued to pay its taxes to the Mongol-Tatars. Secretly, the Slavs were preparing for a fight. The new city of Moscow was their headquarters. A fortress was built, called the Kremlin.

War finally broke out and the Tatars were defeated at Novgorod in 1471 by Ivan III (1462–1505), better known as Ivan the Great. He was the first true national sovereign of Russia. At the time that Columbus entered the "New World,"

Ivan was invading Lithuania. Moscow became the capital of all Russia.

The First Czar

The next king, Ivan IV (1533–1584), was the first Russian sovereign to be crowned czar. Czar is the Russian way of saying "caesar," which was the name given to former Roman emperors who were greatly admired. Ivan's coronation took place in the Uspensky Cathedral, located inside the Kremlin, in Moscow. He inherited the throne when he was only 3 years old. His Lithuanian mother, Helen, ruled in his place for years. Then powerful boyars (nobles) took over until Ivan was 17.

It was rumored that Ivan considered marrying Queen Elizabeth I, the queen of England. Instead he married a Russian girl, Anastasia, from the Romanov family. A hundred years and six kings later, the Romanov dynasty was firmly established. (A dynasty is a succession of rulers from the same family.) Throughout its history, Russia has had only two dynasties, or royal families: the Ruriks and the Romanovs.

Ivan IV was known by another name: Ivan the Terrible. "Terrible" is not the best translation of the Russian word *grozny*, which really means "awesome" ("someone to be revered"). The word also means "someone to be feared or dreaded."

Ivan was a cruel but effective warrior. He liberated the Volga region from marauders. He fought the Swedes in the north and the Livonians, a German tribe, and the Lithuanians

in the west. He was the first Russian monarch to capture new territory in the east, in Siberia. Ivan believed in the "divine right of kings," which meant, to him, that kings could do no wrong and that a ruler always had complete power over his subjects.

Peter the Great

One hundred years would pass before another Russian king like Ivan would appear. His name was Peter, and he would be known as Peter the Great (1682–1725). He would live up to his name.

Peter was a huge man, nearly seven feet tall, and he was curious about everything. Peter learned many useful skills from foreigners, mostly Germans, who lived in Moscow. He established the first fire department and built the first hospital in Russia. Unlike many Russians of his day, he wasn't suspicious of "outsiders."

Peter was the first Russian king to visit the West. He disguised himself and pretended he was just an ordinary tourist, but it was easy for people to guess who this giant really was. He lived in Holland for a time. Later, he worked in an English shipyard. While in England, he visited the British Parliament. He returned to Russia to defeat the Turks and to build a navy.

Like Ivan, Peter could also be very cruel. As a child, when he played toy soldiers, he didn't maneuver toys but ordered human soldiers to act in his games. Often those soldiers were wounded; some were killed. He built a new

Ivan the Terrible

capital, at great human cost, which he named Sankt Peterburg, or St. Petersburg. He made life intolerable for the serfs, who were slave farm workers. He banished his first wife to a convent, a strict religious community for women. In a fit of fury, he once executed a thousand of his best troops in Moscow's Red Square. Peter's own son, Alexis, died in prison. Later in life, Peter adopted the impressive title of Emperor of the Russian Empire.

Catherine II

Peter did not realize his dream of making Russia more European. The pursuit of that goal was continued 37 years later by Catherine the Great (1762–1796).

Catherine II was a German princess (born Sophie of Anhalt-Zerbst) who married Peter the Great's grandson, also named Peter (Peter III). This younger Peter was weak both physically and mentally. After only six months on the throne, he was removed by the army. When he was murdered, his widow, Catherine, became empress.

Catherine, the German princess, truly loved Russia and its language, and her Russian subjects came to adore her. She was responsible for building many new roads and bridges. She encouraged education. She fostered new industries.

Catherine was the first person in Russia to be vaccinated against smallpox, setting an example for her people. She authorized the first Russian settlement in Alaska. She absorbed Ukraine, Crimea, and part of Poland into the Russian

Catherine the Great

empire. She was helped by the cossacks, a hardy group of fun- and freedom-loving cavalrymen from the southern steppe, whose ancestors had been serfs.

Alexander and Napoleon

Following Catherine's death, her son, Paul, was murdered, and her grandson Alexander may have had a hand in the plot.

Nevertheless, Alexander I (1801–1825) tried to improve conditions for the ordinary people. He abolished the secret police and the censorship of newspapers. He released political prisoners. Russian colonies were expanded in Alaska; one was even established in California. He wanted to free the serfs, but this would not happen during his lifetime.

His good intentions were frustrated when he had to fight Napoleon, the emperor of France, who had already conquered Europe. Napoleon attacked Russia in June 1812, with half a million of his best troops. A major battle was fought at Borodino, near Moscow. There were 80,000 casualties. The Russians continued to retreat, burning cities as they went. In September 1812, Napoleon reached Moscow, which was now in ruins, and occupied the Kremlin. Alexander refused Napoleon's offer of peace and decided to fight on.

Napoleon, despite his victory, could not supply his troops with ammunition and food during a harsh and bitter winter. It is said that Napoleon was defeated not so much by Russian troops but by Russia's snow and mud. Now it was Napoleon's turn to retreat—all the way back to France, reaching Paris just before Christmas 1812. Napoleon's war lasted only six months and he had lost 400,000 soldiers. Two years later, Alexander entered Paris with his own troops.

Meanwhile, a group of young Russian army officers openly discussed the need for a constitution, a document that would set down the fundamental principles and rules that would govern their country. They wanted to abolish serfdom, which kept peasant farmers in virtual slavery. They supported land reform, which would give land to those peasant farmers. Some even wanted to end the monarchy and establish a republic.

The First Revolution

Alexander died on December 13, 1825. Since he had no children, his brother Nicholas (1825–1855) was named czar but due to much confusion, his coronation was delayed.

The rebel officers decided that this was the time to overthrow the government. They made their move on December 26, the day after Christmas. This "Decembrist Revolt" was poorly planned and coordinated. Nicholas quickly suppressed the rebellion the day it began. Several army leaders were executed; others were exiled, or banished, to Siberia.

The first revolution had failed.

Nicholas I

Nicholas was the complete opposite of Alexander. During the

30 years of his reign, he would not allow any talk about either a constitution or emancipation of the serfs. Nicholas was a true autocrat—a dictator, a ruler with absolute power. The secret police reappeared, and censorship returned. University life was strictly controlled, Poland was crushed, and Siberia became a giant prison camp for anyone who dared to disagree with the czar.

Alexander II

The son of Nicholas, Alexander II (1855–1881), is called the Czar Liberator because he finally freed the serfs in 1861 (this was two years before slaves were freed in the United States). Alexander organized zemstvos, or local governing councils, which imposed local taxes. Nobles, townspeople, and peasants were represented in these councils. Justices of the peace were appointed to handle local disputes. During his reign, Alaska, which had become a financial burden to Russia, was sold to the United States.

Alexander wanted to liberalize his country, encouraging and expanding local governing bodies with less control from Moscow. However, his reforms came too late or did not go far enough. Many Russians still demanded a written constitution as well as a congress. Alexander II was killed by a terrorist bomb, placed by a radical group called the Will of the People.

The successors to Alexander II would never be as liberal and reasonable as he was. His son, Alexander III (1881–1894), vowed to crush the revolutionaries who had murdered his father. He also began pogroms, which were violent attacks upon the Jews. However, many factories and railroads were built during his reign.

Alexander's son Nicholas II (1894–1917) would be the last czar of Russia. He was an intelligent but weak-willed man.

3. The Communist Experiment

The end of the Romanov monarchy began in 1905, when a general strike was called after a humiliating defeat in the war Russia had been waging against Japan. Many new political parties had been formed and Nicholas II finally proclaimed a constitution and allowed a congress (called the duma) to meet.

Among the political parties was the Social Democratic party, which took its ideas from Karl Marx, a German refugee in England who urged workers to create a communist state. The party split in 1901. The Mensheviks were moderate socialists; the Bolsheviks were extreme radical communists. One of the earliest "Marxist" leaders in Russia was Georgi Plekhanov. His successor was Vladimir Ilyich Ulyanov, who changed his last name to Lenin. Lenin was responsible for calling the general strike of workers.

One result of the strike was political confusion. As each new duma was elected, it changed the decisions of the one it had replaced. This chaos was encouraged by Lenin and other communists. They had little patience for simply making laws. As Karl Marx had taught them, they believed that total revolution, not legislation, was the answer to Russia's problems. World War I (1914-1918) began during this political crisis.

Again, Russia lost important battles, this time against Germany. Czar Nicholas was blamed for the defeats and was

forced to give up the throne, not only for himself, but also for
his son. Michael, Nicholas's brother, refused the crown. A
temporary government was formed. Nicholas and his family
were later murdered by the communists.

Lenin Assumes Power

The provisional, or temporary, government declared Russia
to be a republic, led by the moderate Social Democratic party.
As socialists, the members of this political party favored
government ownership of certain factories and utilities (such
as electric companies). However, socialists did allow private
ownership of property, and they supported democratic
elections. Their chief opponents were communists, the "radical socialists" or Bolsheviks, who insisted that *all* property
should be owned and controlled by the state. Since they
believed that they alone worked for the people, communists
wanted to ban all other political parties.

The temporary government tried very hard to establish a
democracy. It was led first by Prince Georgi Lvov and, later,
by Alexander Kerensky, but this government survived only
seven months. On November 7, 1917, Lenin, with the back-
ing of soldiers, sailors, and workers in Petrograd (the new
name for St. Petersburg), took over the government. He said,
"History will not forgive us if we do not seize power now."

A new election was held and the Bolsheviks received
only 25 percent of the vote. Although they lost the election,
the communists just disbanded the congress. Lenin, with the
help of his Red Guards, again assumed control. His govern-

A reminder of Soviet days: the statue of Lenin in Moscow

ment operated by decree, just as the czars before him had done. All land and factories became the property of the state. Banks were nationalized. Church property was confiscated.

World War I was still being fought, but Lenin made a separate peace with Germany in 1917 (the war itself would continue for another year). Germany's price for peace with Russia was that Russia had to give up the three Baltic states and part of Poland to Germany. Lenin gave Ukraine its independence, for the time being.

The USSR

In 1918 civil war broke out within Russia between the Reds and the Whites. The Reds were the communists; the Whites were those who opposed the communists and wanted to continue the war against Germany. The Red Army won.

In 1922 Russia was joined by Byelorussia (today called Belarus), Transcaucasia, and Ukraine to form the Union of Soviet Socialist Republics (USSR). Eventually, 15 republics would make up this federation. The word Soviet means council; the 1917 revolution had begun with factory "soviets" and farm "soviets." The hammer and sickle on the Soviet Union's red flag symbolized the power of the workers.

The Leaders After Lenin

Lenin died in 1924 but his influence continued throughout the existence of the Soviet Union. He was called the father of his communist country, and his photographs and statues were seen everywhere.

Before Lenin's death, there was a terrible famine (1921–1922) in which many thousands of people died. Herbert Hoover, a future president of the United States, helped to distribute food. However, the United States did not officially recognize the USSR until 1933.

Lenin was followed by Joseph Stalin (1924–1953). He was not a Russian, but was born in Georgia, south of the Caucasus Mountains. His actual name was Joseph Dzhugashvili. He chose the name Stalin because it meant "hard as steel." Stalin was general secretary of the Communist party and became a very harsh dictator.

Huge collective farms (kolkhoz) and state farms

(sovkhoz) were begun in 1928. Kulaks, the wealthier farmers who owned the land and refused to give up their farms, were exiled or killed. The cossack soldiers, who would fight for whoever would pay them, were disarmed. Stalin had many arguments with other communist leaders, and more than a million communists were expelled from the party or were executed.

Stalin made a secret agreement of friendship and non-aggression in 1939 with the German dictator Adolf Hitler. As a result, the Soviet Union was allowed to occupy the three Baltic republics. Germany attacked Poland in 1939, which started World War II, but as part of its agreement with Germany, the Soviet Union remained neutral. Hitler broke his agreement with Stalin in 1941 and invaded the Soviet Union. The German armies now fought on two fronts—in the west (in France and Belgium) and in the east (in the Soviet Union).

The Great Patriotic War

World War II was a tragic time for the Soviet nation. Hitler's army reached the Volga River in the east and the city of Leningrad (formerly called St. Petersburg and Petrograd) in the north. Moscow itself was in danger.

Twenty million Soviet soldiers and civilians were killed in what the Russians called their "great patriotic war." The fighting continued for four years. Military supplies were provided by the Western Allies (chiefly France, Great Britain, and the United States) and eventually the German army,

Leningrad (now St. Petersburg) War Memorial

fighting on two fronts, had to retreat. Many cities and villages were burned as the Nazis returned to Germany.

As the Western Allies pushed east, the Soviet armies marched west and captured Berlin. American GIs met the Soviet soldiers at Torgau, Germany, on the Elbe River, on April 25, 1945. The war ended in Europe two weeks later, on May 8.

Even before the capture of Berlin, the three leaders of the Allied nations had met in Yalta, a Soviet resort on the Black Sea. The Soviet dictator Joseph Stalin, President Franklin Roosevelt of the United States, and Prime Minister Winston Churchill of Britain set terms for Germany's surrender. They redrew the map of Europe. Germany would be divided, with East Germany assigned to the Soviet bloc (group), along with Poland, Czechoslovakia, Hungary, Bulgaria, Romania, and Yugoslavia. This division between East and West continued until the freedom movements of 1989.

The Cold War

The Soviet Union exploded its first atomic bomb in 1949. The partnership of the wartime allies changed to a relationship of mutual suspicion, and an arms race developed between the USSR and the United States.

The Soviet *Sputnik*, the first unmanned space satellite, was launched in 1957 and the space race began between the two superpowers. The Soviet cosmonaut Yuri Gagarin became the first man in space in April 1961. One month later, he was followed by Alan Shepard, the American astronaut.

After Stalin

Georgi Malenkov (1953–1955) and Marshal Nikolai Bulganin (1955–1958) briefly succeeded Stalin until Nikita Khrushchev assumed leadership in 1958.

Khrushchev denounced the terrorism of Stalin and his "cult of personality." Pictures and statues of Joseph Stalin were removed and destroyed. Even the name of Stalingrad, the city where the greatest battle of World War II took place, was changed to Volgograd. Despite these appearances of reform, the weapons buildup continued and Khrushchev proudly declared that communism would, in the end, outlast capitalism.

During Khrushchev's and John F. Kennedy's administrations, the Soviet Union placed ballistic missiles in Cuba. Under pressure from the United States in what was called the Cuban Missile Crisis, Khrushchev finally agreed to remove the missiles.

Khrushchev was ousted by members of his party in 1964.

The Brezhnev Era

Khrushchev was succeeded by Leonid Brezhnev, who held three titles: first secretary of the Communist party, prime minister, and president.

Leonid Brezhnev, born in Ukraine, as was Khrushchev, led the Soviet Union for 18 years. It was a roller coaster period, with highs and lows in foreign relations, punctuated by economic and agricultural disasters. The Strategic Arms Limitation Treaty (SALT) talks began with the United States in 1969, with agreement on some reduction of weapons reached in 1972. Soviet cosmonauts and American astronauts had a historic meeting in space, in 1975, in a joint *Apollo-Soyuz* mission. That same year, the Helsinki Accords were signed in Finland, affirming human rights and greater cooperation between the USSR and the West. During the Brezhnev era, the Soviet Union imported millions of tons of grain from Canada and the United States.

In 1979 the Soviet Union invaded Afghanistan. The United States responded by cancelling its grain shipments and refusing to participate in the 1980 Olympics, which were held in Moscow.

Brezhnev died in 1982. His successor was Yuri Andropov, who ruled for two years. He was the former head of the KGB, the Soviet security or "secret" police. He was succeeded by Konstantin Chernenko, a 72-year-old ally of Brezhnev, who served only one year until his death.

Gorbachev and His Changes

Mikhail Gorbachev assumed power in 1985, first as chairman of the Communist party, then prime minister, and eventually as president of the Soviet Union.

Gorbachev was 54 years old when he became the leader of the USSR This was considered young by Soviet standards. His predecessors had all been older men who had known Stalin personally, and who had fought during World War II.

Gorbachev brought a fresh viewpoint. He had not known Stalin. He was too young to have fought during World War II. He was the first Soviet leader to have had a university education, and he received degrees in both law and agriculture. Like all good communists, Gorbachev did not profess to believe in God. However, as an infant he had been baptized in the Russian Orthodox church, and he was sympathetic to the church. He understood the power of the media and became an effective and energetic politician.

At the 27th Communist Party Congress in 1986, Gorbachev announced his program of glasnost and perestroika. His plan was to transform the Soviet Union totally.

His concepts did bring change. They also brought about the end of the Soviet Union itself.

Glasnost

Glasnost is the Russian word for "openness." It came to mean freedom of speech, freedom to get information, freedom from propaganda. It meant that Soviet citizens would have the right to travel and emigrate to other countries, although this right was not approved by the Congress until 1991.

Filmmakers produced documentaries about the mistakes and crimes of earlier Soviet leaders. TV cameras brought *live* coverage of the proceedings of the Congress. For the first time, press conferences forced officials to explain and defend their policies. The entire nation began to see what democracy looked like.

The "prisoners of conscience," those who had criticized or defied the old system, were released from prisons and work camps. Among them were writers, members of the clergy, rabbis, teachers, and scientists. One of them, the late Andrei Sakharov, a famous nuclear physicist, was elected to the Congress.

The war with Afghanistan was ended.

Glasnost did indeed bring change. There would be no turning back.

Perestroika

Perestroika, Gorbachev's second policy challenge, is the

Russian word for "restructuring." It also means renewal or reformation, rebuilding, reshaping, redesigning, "turning things around." Combined with glasnost, perestroika invited Soviet citizens to participate in the decisions that would affect their future. It encouraged the questioning of old authority, of the ways things had been done in the past; it invited citizens to debate plans handed down "from the top." Perestroika was nothing less than a new revolution.

In his book about the movement, Gorbachev defined it as "a thorough renewal of every aspect of Soviet life." He said that this change had to be economic, social, political, and moral. He said he wanted to develop democracy, encourage private enterprise, and improve working and living conditions for Soviet citizens.

In foreign relations, Gorbachev declared that the cold war was over. The Berlin Wall was toppled. Communist leaders were overthrown in Poland, Hungary, Romania, Bulgaria, Czechoslovakia, and East Germany. However, when the freedom movement surfaced in Soviet republics, Gorbachev sent troops to contain the rebels. Nearly two dozen people, some of them teenagers, were shot or run over by tanks in Lithuania and Latvia.

The Revolt against Gorbachev

In August 1991, Mikhail Gorbachev and his wife, Raisa, went to Crimea, on the Black Sea, for a vacation. In his absence, several of his closest associates staged a coup, or mutiny. They included his vice president, the prime minister, the head of the KGB (the security police), and the ministers (or secretaries) of defense, foreign affairs, and the interior. They felt that President Gorbachev had gone too far with his ideas of reform and that communism itself was at risk. The revolt lasted only 72 hours. The armed forces refused to obey the orders of the military leaders who supported the coup. One of the rebel leaders committed suicide.

Gorbachev returned to Moscow shaken and offended by what had been done by people he had considered to be his friends.

The Soviet Union was dissolved in early December of 1991. And so was the Communist party. On Christmas Day 1991, Mikhail Gorbachev resigned as president of the Soviet Union.

The Third Revolution and Boris Yeltsin

The hero of the August uprising was Boris Nikolayevich Yeltsin. As president of Russia, he challenged the rebel leaders who wanted to overthrow Gorbachev. He remained within the Russian Parliament building, which Moscow citizens called the White House, throughout the three days of rebellion. When the Parliament building was surrounded by tanks and troops, he climbed on top of one of the tanks to rally the soldiers and the citizens to support democracy, calling for a general strike.

Yeltsin and Gorbachev were the same age. Yeltsin was born in Siberia, near Sverdlovsk (now called Yekaterinburg), east of the Ural Mountains, in 1931. He became a civil

A rare meeting: Gorbachev and Yeltsin shake hands

engineer. He and Gorbachev were both loyal communists and had once been good friends. In fact, Yeltsin was named the Communist party boss for the city of Moscow. However, in time Yeltsin became impatient with the slow pace of reform and unhappy with the Communist party. He openly began to criticize the Soviet leader.

The break between the two men came in 1987. Yeltsin was forced to leave the party's Central Committee, the power center of the Soviet government. Meanwhile, however, Yeltsin had become a kind of folk hero. People liked his frank talk and peasant mannerisms. His favorite food, it was reported, was herring and boiled potatoes. Because of glasnost, he was frequently seen on television. He was popular not only in Moscow but throughout the Soviet Union.

Two years later, he sought the post of deputy-at-large for Congress, representing the city of Moscow. The Communist party did everything it could to defeat him. Many people compared Yeltsin to David, fighting a giant Goliath. However, he won by a landslide; five million people voted for him, 89.4 percent of the entire vote. He was reelected in 1990 and was made chairman of the Supreme Soviet, the chief legislative body of the Soviet Union. He resigned from the Communist party and convinced Congress to declare that Russian laws had priority over Soviet laws. This was a dramatic challenge to the old administration.

In 1991 Yeltsin ran for the presidency of the Russian republic and won with 60 percent of the vote. He was the first popularly elected leader in Russian history. His election was a personal defeat for Mikhail Gorbachev, who had campaigned against Yeltsin.

The future of the Soviet Union was very much in doubt later that year with the eruption of the August revolt. There was talk of a new confederation of sovereign states, then of some kind of economic union that would allow each former Soviet republic to manage its own political affairs.

On December 8, 1991, the new leaders of Russia, Ukraine, and Belarus met in the city of Minsk and declared that the

Soviet Union had ceased to exist. They proclaimed a new Commonwealth of Independent States, which all former members of the Soviet Union were invited to join. This action effectively took away the power and authority of Gorbachev, who no longer had a country to govern.

Seven former Soviet republics soon joined the new Commonwealth, which now has ten members.

4. Getting to Know the Russian People

The Russian Sense of Humor

Survival in Russia has always required a sense of humor and patience.

When rules and regulations were determined by the orders of the local boyar, or nobleman, or by the local communist commissar, a person could not openly protest inequality or injustice. People had to be very careful. Often their criticism of the government took the form of humorous stories. Sometimes the stories used irony, or "double meaning," to make their point. Here's an example:

When Catherine the Great captured Crimea, in southern Russia, she wanted new villages built and settled as quickly as possible. She instructed her friend Grigori Potemkin to proceed with the work. Potemkin had neither sufficient settlers nor materials to carry out the order. So he built fake structures—false fronts that faced the street with absolutely nothing behind them. When Catherine came to inspect her new "villages," riding past them quickly, she had no idea how she was being fooled. What she saw were nothing more than what we would call stage or movie sets. And today, when Russians talk about government statistics or plans being "just for show," they call them "Potemkin villages."

Here are other examples with a touch of humor:

A man went to a doctor's office.

"I must see an ear-and-eye doctor!" he shouted.

"But, old man," said the nurse. "This is just an emergency clinic."

"So this is an emergency! I must see an ear-and-eye doctor. Quickly!"

"Why?"

"Because what I hear every day from the government is not what I see."

❖❖❖

A Russian mother walks into a store filled with empty shelves.

"I see you have no bread," says the shopper to the clerk.

"You are wrong, lady. We sell fish in this store. We have no fish. The store that has no bread is in the next block."

❖❖❖

Here is a story that went the rounds after Mikhail Gorbachev announced his program of perestroika, or restructuring the economy:

A man is demonstrating to another the meaning of perestroika. He has two pails. One pail is empty and the other is full of potatoes. He pours the potatoes from one pail into the other, and is very satisfied with what he is doing.

"But nothing has changed!" declares the second man.

"Of course," agrees the first man, "but think what a noise it makes!"

Patriotism and the Russian "Soul"

Russians are not ashamed to be patriotic. They truly love their *rodina*, or motherland. Within this century, Russians have endured two world wars, a civil war, and a war in Afghanistan. That last 11-year war has been compared to the American involvement in Vietnam, with many casualties and no clear-cut victory. Russians honor their warriors with monuments, holidays, and songs.

Throughout their history, Russians have had reason to fear foreign invasion, and the communist government encouraged that fear. However, fear of foreigners as possible spies or future invaders has practically disappeared with the policy of glasnost.

Today Russians like to practice speaking English. They are delighted with visitors' attempts to speak Russian. They love to talk and ask questions.

Russians have always been generous and like to be good hosts. A visitor must be careful not to admire too enthusiastically something in a Russian's home or some-thing a Russian is wearing; the Russian host may want to give that item to the visitor to keep, especially if the visitor is a foreigner. Russians like to share food and give presents. In former days, before inflation and unemploy-ment, a Russian family might spend an entire week's salary to splurge on a lavish restaurant meal with friends of the family.

Russians are sentimental. You see tears and lots of embracing and kissing in railroad stations or airports, as family members say farewell to one another. It's an old

Russians and Americans share friendship in Uzbekistan

Russian custom for men to kiss men, whether in greeting or saying "good-bye." You don't joke about it.

Literature

Russians are readers, perhaps because Russia has produced so many outstanding writers. These writers include Feodor Dostoyevsky, who spent nine years in Siberia as a convict and soldier. One of his more famous works is *Crime and Punishment*. Count Leo Tolstoy wrote *War and Peace*, which dealt with Napoleon's invasion of Russia. Alexander Pushkin has been compared to William Shakespeare. Pushkin wrote novels, poetry, and children's stories; one of his children's stories is "The Golden Cockerel." Boris Pasternak wrote *Doctor Zhivago*. Alexander Solzhenitsyn wrote *The*

Gulag Archipelago; he won the Nobel Prize in literature in 1970. Other Russian writers who received this high award for literature are Ivan Bunin (1933), Boris Pasternak (1958; he declined the prize), and Mikhail Sholokhov (1965). Many libraries offer works by these Russian writers in English translations.

Music

Russians love music. It doesn't matter whether it's piano or violin concertos, symphonies, string quartets, folk songs, rock, or ballet. Even small cities have concert halls.

Some of Russia's leading composers are Alexander Borodin, Sergei Prokofiev, Modest Mussorgsky, Igor Stravinsky, Nikolai Rimsky-Korsakov, Dmitri Shostakovich, and Pyotr Ilyich Tchaikovsky. Tchaikovsky wrote the *1812 Overture*, inspired by Napoleon's invasion of Russia and his defeat. In this composition, you hear fragments of the national anthems of both Russia and France, colliding with each other. You can also hear cannon fire, symbolizing the battles that brought about Napoleon's downfall.

Jazz and rock and roll were banned by the communists but Russia now has many groups playing these forms of popular music.

Religion

The Russians are a deeply religious and spiritual people. Although the Soviet Union officially discouraged religious

A traditional Russian entertainment: folk dancing

worship, the church survived and grew. Many churches were confiscated by the communists and transformed into museums, movie houses, concert halls, and warehouses. These houses of worship are now being returned to the "believers."

The Russian Orthodox church is the largest religious community. Its steeples look like inverted tulip bulbs or onions and dot the landscape of both cities and countryside. The Orthodox church has preserved the ancient Slavic language in its worship. Its art, seen in icons and heard in its liturgy and its beautiful unaccompanied singing, continues to influence the Russian character. The Russian Orthodox church celebrated its 1,000th birthday in 1988. Bibles, once banned, and other religious literature are being printed without restriction.

Other Christian groups include Adventists, Baptists, Lutherans, Mennonites, Pentecostals, and Roman Catholics.

Jews are again allowed to study Hebrew, and yeshivas are being established. Jews are no longer prohibited from emigrating to Israel, if they so choose.

The Muslim population is found largely in the central Asian republics of the Commonwealth, but there are Muslims in Russia. Many of them are Tatars who live near the Volga River. Stalin closed 26,000 mosques, but Islam, along with the other religions, survived and is growing.

Buddhists in Russia live among the Buryat, Tiwan, and Kalmyk tribes in central Asia.

The Secret Behind Russian Names

Russian names aren't easy to pronounce but they give us lots

A Russian wedding

of information about the person to whom they belong.

To explain, let's analyze the full name of Boris Niko-layevich Yeltsin.

Boris is his given (or first) name.

The second name, Nikolayevich, is called a "patrony-mic," which is common in Russia and indicates relationship to one's father. *Nikolayevich* means "son of Nikolai (or Nicholas)." Thus, his name is "Boris, son of Nikolai." We follow the same pattern in English, although we don't use patronymics in the same way. Stevenson, for example, once meant "the son of Steven." O'Reilly to Irish persons meant "the son of Reilly."

Yeltsin is the family name, which indicates he is a man. Married women have distinctive endings to the family name. Mrs. Yeltsin would be known as Yeltsinova.

Many of the given names are recognizable even without knowing Russian. Ivan is John. Yuri, or Yurgi, is George. Pavel is Paul. Feodor is Francis. Sonia is Sonia, but its origin is the Greek name Sophronia. Alya is Alice. Katerina is Catherine. Konstantin is Constantine. Lisenka is Elizabeth.

Some of the given names are distinctively Russian. Tatiana, a girl's name, honors a third-century martyr of the church. Anastasia honors another martyr; this name, in Greek, means "resurrection."

Russian parents love to use names, or nicknames, of affection for their children. These special names are called "diminutives" and we have them in English, too. Johnny is a diminutive of John; Betty (Elizabeth) and Peggy (Margaret) are other examples. You will see many Russian diminutives as you read English translations of Russian novels and short stories. Misha is the familiar form of Michael. Other examples: Vanya (John), Sasha (Alexei), Katya (Catherine), Tosha (Anthony), and Tanya (Tatiana).

The Russian Language

Russian is a Slavic language and uses the Cyrillic alphabet. It is easy to read and speak Russian once you learn these new letters of the alphabet, because Russian is always spelled phonetically, just the way it sounds. Here are several phrases you may want to learn and try out on your friends. They are written phonetically, using Latin letters.

ZDRAS-tvooy-tyee?—"How do you do?"
kahk-dyee-LAH?—"How are you?"
khah-rah-SHOW!—"Fine!"
spah-SEE-bah.—"Thank you."
pah-ZHAH-loo-stah.—"Please."

Equality and Democracy

Throughout Russia's history there have been two classes of people. There were the haves and the have nots. There were those who owned land and those who did not; those who governed and those who were governed. Another division was the intelligentsia (literally, "the intelligent ones") and the muzhiki (or "peasants"); thus there were those who had an education and those who did not.

The intellectuals came from privileged families. Only the very rich could afford higher education. In the time of the czars, many intellectuals preferred to speak French rather than Russian. Often they seemed embarrassed to be known as Russians.

Serfs were once literally enslaved to their masters. Although they could not read or write, they had a deep love for their land and their language. The peasants were proud to be Slavs and speak Russian; they helped keep their language alive.

Officially there were no distinctions among people during the era of the Soviet Union. The communists proclaimed a "classless" society. Yet there were differences. Highly placed persons in the government or the military enjoyed special privileges—their own stores where they could buy hard-to-get items, comfortable apartments, cars, and sometimes vacation homes called dachas. Cosmonauts, engineers, scientists, and favored artists, musicians, and writers often also enjoyed the same advantages.

Under the czars, the king was called the "little father," and was to be obeyed, no matter how cruel he might be. Under communism, the commissars, or leaders, demanded a similar obedience. But changing times are challenging this legacy of the past.

As Russia returns to a free market economy, there may again be a return to economic classes. There will be those who are richer and there will be those who are poorer. However, democracy has also come to Russia. Education was free to everyone under the Soviets. Education continues to be available to anyone. People are free to change jobs and to improve their situation. It is hoped that success will not be determined by birth or birthplace or the status of one's parents, but by one's ability and energy. Because of glasnost and perestroika, as well as the collapse of communism, Russian citizens are discovering that people can truly have both power and a voice in their own destiny.

That power and voice were expressed in December 1993, when Russian citizens approved Yeltsin's proposed constitution, which grants the president greater power to govern.

Voters, however, did not give Mr. Yeltsin the majority he would have liked in the new duma, or congress. Russians elected a few former communists, several royalists (who support a return to a monarchy), and many "far right" members of a "Liberal Democratic Party," led by lawyer Vladimir V. Zhirinovsky, an anti-Jewish nationalist.

The election was preceded by a military confrontation between Yeltsin and the former congress.

A new presidential election is scheduled for 1996.

5. Cities and Beyond

Moscow

If you were asked to name the most important city in Russia, you would probably answer Moscow. It's called "mosk-VAH" in Russian. It is Russia's capital and its largest city, with nearly nine million people.

Moscow is the city most Russians like to visit. It is a center of government and education, and it's a popular place to shop. Moscow is the entertainment capital of Russia, home of the internationally famous Bolshoi Opera and Ballet company, the Moscow Circus, and dozens of theaters.

Moscow is known for the Kremlin, which is a Russian word meaning "fortress" or "citadel." Moscow's first kremlin was begun in 1367, but because of fires and wars it has been rebuilt many times. Situated on a hill overlooking the Moscow River, its walls form a triangle.

Those walls were designed and built by Italian architects in the 15th century during the reign of Ivan III. The walls are 1½ miles (2.4 kilometers) in circumference, 20 feet (6 meters) thick, and 65 feet (20 meters) high. Within its walls are many churches, palaces, an armory, towers, and government buildings.

The oldest church within the Kremlin is the Assumption (Uspensky) Cathedral, built in 1479. It was the place where the czars were crowned. Ivan the Terrible's magnificent carved throne can still be seen there.

Russians and foreign tourists visit the Kremlin to see its ancient treasures and art. The Great Bell Tower, built by Ivan the Great and enlarged by Boris Godunov, is a major attraction. It was once the tallest building in Moscow, rising to 266 feet (81 meters). There are 73 bells in the belfry, two of which weigh more than 60 tons. At the tower's base is the largest bell in the world, weighing 200 tons. It is called the Czar Bell. It once hung in the tower but cracked during a fire in 1737 and has now been removed and placed on the ground.

Not everything within the Kremlin is old. The Palace of Congresses was built in 1960 and is an ultramodern glass-and-aluminum structure. Some Russians think it is out of place and call it a giant aquarium.

One of the squares facing the Kremlin is Red Square. The Russian word for "red" is *krasnaya*, which also means "beautiful." This is the largest public square in the world and was the site of huge military parades during the Soviet era.

Next to the Kremlin wall on Red Square is Lenin's Mausoleum. Russian doctors found a way to embalm Vladimir Lenin's body and place it in a glass casket so that people could continue to see the founder of the communist state. The red granite structure became a shrine. Now that communism no longer controls Russia, deputies in the Congress are suggesting that Lenin be given a proper burial elsewhere.

On the same square is St. Basil's Cathedral, built by Ivan the Terrible in 1552 to celebrate his defeat of the Tatars. This is one of the strangest and most colorful churches anywhere

The Arbat shopping section of Moscow

in the world. Eight small chapels are covered by eight swirly onion-bulb-shaped domes that look like soft ice-cream cones. The interior is decorated with bright flowers. Tradition says that after the cathedral was built, Ivan blinded the architects so they could never again build such a beautiful structure.

Also on Red Square is the GUM department store. The letters, in Russian, stand for "State Department Store." This three-story shopping mall was built in 1894. There are more than 1½ miles (2.4 kilometers) of stores and boutiques under its glass-and-metal domed roof. Nearby is the 21-story Rossiya (Russia) Hotel with 3,000 rooms.

The State Library, near the Kremlin, contains 30 million books. There are several huge reading rooms, where up to

2,500 people can read at tables at one time. Ten thousand visitors come each day to read and do research. Books must be read in the library and cannot be checked out.

There is a "new" Moscow with wide avenues and tall buildings. To get to the Olympic Stadium or the Moscow State University, you can travel quickly by subway trains. Moscow's subway system is clean and efficient, the trains run every three minutes, and the stations are decorated with beautiful tiled mosaics and are illuminated by chandeliers.

St. Petersburg

This city, on the Gulf of Finland, was begun by Peter the Great in 1703. In 1712 he declared it to be the new capital of the Russian empire. Peter wanted to open a window to Europe and the West, and believed it was necessary to move the capital from Moscow closer to the Baltic Sea. He forced the nobility to move and live in his new city. Finland is only 90 miles (145 kilometers) away. The capital was moved back to Moscow in 1918.

St. Petersburg was built on marshland on a delta of 40 islands formed by the Neva River. Today it is a beautiful city, which many people compare with Paris because of its formal architecture and elegant ironwork and streetlamps. Others compare it with Amsterdam or Venice because of its many canals and bridges.

St. Petersburg's name was changed to Petrograd (the city of Peter) in 1914. Ten years later, its name was changed to Leningrad, to honor the death and memory of Vladimir I.

St. Petersburg's Winter Palace

Lenin, who led the communist revolution, and to honor the city that was known as "the cradle of the revolution."

During World War II, the Nazis surrounded the city and laid siege to it for nearly three years. The Nazi effort to subdue the city is famous in history as the Siege of Leningrad. A million people died from starvation, a third of the population. Getting enough food through the German blockade, across the salt marshes, is one of history's great stories of adventure and courage. A memorial cemetery honors those who died.

In 1991 Leningrad's citizens voted to restore the city's original name: Sankt Peterburg (St. Petersburg). St. Petersburg is Russia's second-largest city, with some five million inhabitants, and it is a major trading and shipbuilding center. Factories produce textiles, generators, and tractors.

St. Petersburg's main avenue is Nevsky Prospekt, named for Alexander Nevsky, who, in this very region, defeated the Swedes in the 13th century. A famous monastery, built by Peter the Great, is also named for this hero.

Two cathedrals are noteworthy. The Kazan (kah-ZAHN), on Nevsky Prospekt, has a colonnade similar to St. Peter's in Rome. This is where royal children were baptized. Another cathedral is St. Isaac's, whose dome can be seen from most of the city, and from which you can see most of St. Petersburg. It took 40 years to complete and was built by serf labor. It was finished in 1842 and was the site of royal weddings.

The Peter and Paul Fortress (St. Peterburg's kremlin) was the first structure to be built in the city. Peter, who built it, is buried there. So is Feodor Dostoyevsky, the author, who lived in St. Petersburg and who was imprisoned briefly in the fortress.

The Hermitage is a world-famous art museum, housed in what was once the Winter Palace of the czars. It was designed by the Italian architect Rastrelli. The museum contains art treasures from the imperial collection, as well as works confiscated by the communists from private collections.

There is also a Summer Palace, located outside the city, built by Peter the Great. It copies the design of the palace at Versailles, in France.

For entertainment, there is the world-class Philharmonic Orchestra and the Kirov Opera and Ballet. During the "white nights" of summer, when there is daylight until midnight, musical and dramatic performances can be seen throughout the city. There are impressive fireworks displays. There is also a famous puppet theater and, as in most larger Russian

The Kirov theater, St. Petersburg

cities, an indoor year-round circus. Boat trips along the canals are always popular.

Novosibirsk

Novosibirsk (pronounced "novo-see-BEERSK," which means "new Siberia") is Siberia's largest city, with nearly two million inhabitants.

It was created in 1893 as a railroad town where the Trans-Siberian railroad crosses the Ob River. Railroading is still important to span the vast distances of Russia. A school to train railroad engineers is located here.

Novosibirsk is a young and fresh city and an important commercial center. It is laid out like a huge checkerboard, with streets that run vertically and horizontally.

Novosibirsk is the gateway to Siberia, the newest frontier of Russia. Some are calling it the "wild east"! It has rich coal, petroleum, and mineral resources, including diamonds, gold, nickel, tungsten, and iron. Drilling and mining operations continue around the clock.

Much has been written about the "Siberian salt mines" to which Russian prisoners were once sent. There were many prison work camps in Siberia, but no salt mines. This region contains 25 percent of the world's known oil and gas reserves and 50 percent of the world's coal.

Novosibirsk boasts a civic theater that seats more people than the much more famous Bolshoi Theater in Moscow. Its sports arena holds 80,000. The city has its own ballet company, a circus, and a symphony orchestra.

Summers are hot and brief. The temperature climbs to 90° F (32° C), which doesn't sound at all like Siberia. However, winter temperatures drop to -50° F (-45.5° C), and snow is measured in yards (or meters), not in feet.

Twenty miles (32 kilometers) south of Novosibirsk is a "satellite city" called Akademgorodok (pronounced "ah-ka-DYEM-go-ro-DOCK"). This is a sparkling new "science city" where hundreds of scientists work in 22 research centers. These scientists do computer research or work in chemistry, genetics, thermal and nuclear physics, medicine, and space technology. Important conferences and trade fairs are held in its Hall of Sciences.

Life Beyond the Cities

One out of ten Russians lives in a village and most likely is a farmer. Formerly these agricultural workers worked and lived on large collective farms that were owned by the government. Some of them were allowed to keep cows and raise vegetables in a small garden. The collective farms are being transformed into cooperative farms, in which the farmers will share ownership. Breaking up the large farms to reestablish smaller farms is being debated in the Congress.

However, even today farmers do not live on individual farms but in villages, as Russian farmers have done throughout Russian history. Most villages have about 200 people. Their wooden houses, called izbas, line both sides of a single street, which may be paved with cobblestones or asphalt or may still be unpaved.

Summers are short and are filled with planting and harvesting. Winters are long and cold, and farm families spend their time repairing tools and farm equipment, cutting wood, building furniture, weaving cloth, visiting neighbors, or watching television.

Most villages have electricity. They are linked to cities by 530,000 miles (855,000 kilometers) of roads, of which only 387,500 miles (625,100 kilometers) are paved. The unpaved roads become thick with mud in the spring and fall—the result of melting snow or falling rain. In the winter, they are packed with snow, and the best way to travel is by horse and sleigh.

Few villagers can afford to own their own cars. Depending upon the weather, they travel to the nearest city by horse and cart (or sleigh), bicycle, bus, or, perhaps, by train.

Life in the villages can be isolated and monotonous, which is why the cities are such popular places to visit.

6. All in the Family

What is it like to be a member of a Russian family?

First of all, a child will probably have only one brother or one sister. Most Russian families are small by choice and economic conditions.

Housing

In the cities, most Russian families live in high-rise apartment buildings. They are 6 to 14 stories high. Only the taller ones have elevators.

The apartments are small. Ideally, a family will have two bedrooms, a combination living-dining room, a tiny kitchen, and a divided bathroom. The toilet and the bath are in separate closet-size rooms. Sometimes two families have to share the same apartment or parents or grandparents live with the family as well. There isn't much room to move around. Sofa beds are often used for sleeping, since they can provide more space in the daytime.

The more modern apartment buildings are built in clusters, and look very much alike. Sometimes each building has one outside wall or its balcony panels painted in a distinctive color, which makes it easier to find where you live. Heat and hot water come from a central plant; hot water may not always be available every day. Shopping centers are built nearby.

Wealthier people own dachas as well as their condominium-apartment. Dachas are vacation cottages near lakes or forests. Many Russians lease or own small garden plots outside the city, about a quarter acre in size. They plant fruit trees and grow vegetables. They construct greenhouses out of plastic sheeting to protect tender crops and to extend the growing season. They may also build small cabins on their garden plots, where they spend their weekends.

Appliances

Each apartment has a small refrigerator and a gas stove. Some families have tiny portable washing machines, which are placed over the bathtubs. Clothing, however, is usually washed by hand; public Laundromats and clothes dryers are rare. Clothes are dried inside bathrooms or on outside balconies, if available. Vacuum cleaners are also rare. Rugs are beaten on frames made of pipe, which are located outside the buildings.

Television and radio are popular forms of family entertainment. Under the Soviet system, all programs were under government control, although there was a selection of networks and stations. Commercial privately owned stations are now being licensed. Some popular American TV shows are now shown in Russia.

Stereos and portable "boom boxes" are common, as are

audiocassettes and records, but only 11 out of 100 Russian families have a telephone in their homes.

Family Transportation

Russia has a large automotive industry. There is only one "brand," but cars come in different sizes. Limousines, favored by government officials, are called Zils. Intermediate-size cars are called Chaikas, Zhigulis, and Volgas. A compact, built by the Italian company Fiat, is called a Moskovich. Automobiles made in Europe are being imported. All cars are expensive. Roads are not crowded. There are 24 cars for every thousand Russians, compared with 526 cars for every thousand Americans.

Families travel by bus, or they might fly in the Tupolev-designed jet aircraft of Aeroflot, Russia's only domestic airline. If they travel on vacations outside of Russia, they can choose many other airlines that offer international service.

Families might choose the railroad instead. There are many excellent passenger trains in Russia. The most famous is the Trans-Siberian express, which takes eight days to cross 5,000 miles (8,000 kilometers). The ticket price depends on whether one chooses "hard seat" or "soft seat" coaches. Sleeping berths are available on long-distance trips. Trains are driven by diesel or electrical power.

An exciting choice for family vacation travel is an excursion steamer or hydrofoil. These ships sail on many of the larger rivers and lakes.

In major cities, people who don't have a car may choose

either subways, buses, electric buses, electric trolleys, or taxis.

Vacations

Since both parents often have to work, vacations are important times for families. There are many choices: swimming at the seashore of the Baltic, Black, or Caspian seas; hiking in mountains or forests; renting an izba, or cabin; tent camping; visiting one of the bigger cities to sightsee, to see museums, or watch the circus, the ballet, or a puppet show.

Something families often do together is gather mushrooms in the forests. Russian parents have learned from their own parents which mushrooms are edible and which may be poisonous. Mushrooms are usually air-dried and stored for later use. Mushrooms are used a lot in Russian cooking.

Money

Since the days of the czars, Russians have purchased things with rubles and kopeks. There are 100 kopeks in a ruble. The word ruble originally meant "a block of wood"; perhaps the early coins were something like "wooden nickels." The word kopek means "lance." The earliest kopek coins, similar to a penny, show the czar riding a horse and carrying a lance. Kopeks today have no value except as collectors' items.

During the Soviet era, the ruble could not be exchanged for other currency elsewhere in the world. The ruble was called "soft currency." Dollars, British pounds, German

St. Petersburg natives seek out the sun.

marks, Swiss and French francs, and Japanese yen were "hard currency" and much in demand. The new Russian government is working with the World Bank and Western nations to make its ruble stronger and accepted around the world.

Meanwhile, Russia suffers from severe inflation. This means that prices may jump as much as ten times in a year, and keep on climbing. Wages, on the other hand, may increase only two or three times during the same period. What one earns does not keep pace with what one must spend.

The prices of bread and milk are kept low by the government, which pays part of the costs. However, other food products are becoming very expensive—especially meat and cheese.

A good pair of shoes costs the equivalent of an average Russian's monthly salary. Most Russians would have to work five years to earn the money to buy a new subcompact car.

Although rents are also increasing, rents and utilities are partially subsidized by the government and cost less than in the West. Medical costs are also lower because Russia continues to have a national health insurance plan. Nevertheless, "getting along" is difficult for many Russians, particularly for elderly people living on small pensions, and for the increasing numbers of people who are without jobs.

Shopping

Shopping is always an adventure, because you may have to visit many different stores to find the things you need. There are supermarkets for food, but sometimes the shelves are empty. The same is often true in department stores. There are separate places to buy bread, meat, and fish. There are farmers' markets where you will find vegetables, poultry, and flowers. Often people set up shop on sidewalks or street corners to sell vegetables they have grown in their own gardens. Or they may sell expensive fruit like bananas or oranges that they purchased from an importer. Merchants in sidewalk booths, or kiosks, sell drinks, newspapers, and even clothes. These are like convenience stores.

Everyone carries a tiny "string bag" in a pocket or purse, in order to have something in which to carry home a last-minute purchase. Plastic sacks are sold, not given away. Paper bags are very rare.

Huge flea markets are becoming popular. These are like mammoth garage sales, where people bring whatever they have to sell. Thousands of people come to find the automobile part they need, a used stereo, clothing, or kitchen utensils. There might even be something brand-new, not to be found in the stores, that someone brought back from a foreign trip. Some of the items may be stolen goods, so buyers must be cautious.

If you are lucky enough to have foreign currency, there are special stores where you can buy VCRs, automobile tires, coffee, stylish clothes, and other luxury things.

Holidays

Major religious holidays are once again celebrated in Russia. Christmas, Epiphany (January 6), and Easter are important festivals for Christians.

Christmas is a traditional time for worship. The exchange of gifts takes place on New Year's Day, or on Epiphany, which recalls the coming of the wise men with their gifts to see the baby Jesus.

Easter is a time for special festivity. Special foods are prepared—especially cakes and cookies—which are enjoyed long after Easter. A special Easter cake is called *koulich*. It looks like white cake, but has lots of raisins, chopped nuts, and candied fruits. It is frosted and the letters *KV* are etched into the icing.

KV stands for *Khristos Voskress*, and these Russian words mean "Christ Is Risen." On Easter Sunday, Russian

Residents of Moscow still must often stand in line to buy the simplest goods.

Christians greet each other with those words. One will say, "*Khristos voskress!*" and the other will reply, "*Voistinu voskress!*" ("He is risen indeed!").

Another Easter custom is to decorate eggs, called *pysanky*. The eggs are neither cooked nor blown out, but will eventually dry out. Beeswax and many brilliant dyes are used. The beeswax is melted, sometimes with a lighted candle, and dripped onto the egg. A small writing instrument, called a *kistka*, is used to carve the wax or to draw lines or symbols. Typical symbols are ribbons, a fish, the cross, a triangle, and a star. The egg is dipped into the dye; the part of shell still covered by wax will not be affected. More carving on the wax is done, and the egg is again

A young Russian displays decorated eggs, known as pysanky.

placed in the dye, but this time using another color. A finished design may require a dozen layers of wax and several dyes.

Children enjoy learning to decorate eggs. It is an art that requires much time and patience as well as practice and skill. Decorated eggs are given as Easter gifts and displayed throughout the year.

As they do everywhere, Jews celebrate Chanukah, Yom Kippur, and Passover. Chanukah commemorates the liberation of the temple by the Maccabees, in Jerusalem. It continues for eight days, usually in December, and children receive gifts. Yom Kippur announces the New Year. Passover remembers the exodus of the Hebrews from Egypt.

Muslims celebrate the ninth month of their calendar, or Ramadan. This is a time of fasting and meditation, from sunrise to sunset, every day for 28 days. It ends with a feast and exchange of gifts.

The Russian Winter Festival lasts 12 days, from December 25 to January 6. The days are filled with winter sports, carnivals, and special circus performances. Decorated Christmas trees are displayed. A man with a red suit and long white beard is also seen—but he's called Dyed Maroz, or "Grandfather Frost," not Santa Claus.

In June, "White Nights" are celebrated in St. Petersburg with music and drama. These are the longest days of the year, and in the far north the sun does not set until almost midnight.

There are public holidays, of course. May 1 is May Day

and is Russia's Labor Day, honoring farmers and factory workers. This socialist holiday is celebrated in many countries of the world. In Russia it's a day for family fun, for parades, and for making huge statues or puppets out of papier-mâché.

The Soviet Union celebrated November 7 as Revolution Day, and communists still gather for demonstrations. However, the new Russia celebrates June 8 as the day in 1990 when it declared its independence from the laws and government of the Soviet Union. It also commemorates December 8 as the day in 1991 when the new Commonwealth of Independent States was established.

Flowers

Russians love flowers. If they are lucky enough to have a garden, they will use some space to grow their own flowers. Flowers are also grown commercially in hothouses. Kiosks, or sidewalk stands, offer flowers for sale throughout the year.

Flowers are given to celebrate birthdays and anniversaries. They are given to a hostess as a hospitality gift. A single flower is taken to weddings and given to the bride and groom in the reception line. Flowers are given to favorite performers at concerts. Flowers are given singly, or by threes or fives, always in odd numbers. Giving flowers in even numbers is considered bad luck.

7. What's on the Table?

Russians like to eat, and Russian families try to share one or two family meals each day. On holidays, or for family anniversaries, they may go to a restaurant. McDonald's has opened a huge fast-food outlet in Moscow, which is very popular. Pizza has also arrived.

What do Russian people drink and eat?

Beverages

There is milk. There is kvass, a nonalcoholic drink made from dried-out rye bread and yeast, which tastes a bit like root beer. There is seltzer water (called "gassy water" in Russian), which is sold in vending machines. Cola and other soft drinks are sold. Vodka is strictly for adults and is a strong alcoholic drink. Vodka is distilled from rye or barley malt; cheaper grades are made from corn or potatoes. Other adult beverages are beer and wine.

The most popular drink, both for adults and children, is tea. Usually it's brewed and served from a samovar, which is a fancy metal container used to boil water and keep it warm. Charcoal is burned in a self-contained cylinder inside the samovar, or an electric immersion heater heats the water. A small teapot rests on top of the samovar and contains very strong brewed tea. Just a little bit of this "essence" is poured into a cup or glass, and hot water is added from the samovar. Samovars are used everywhere, even on trains.

Tea is usually served in glasses, but never as iced tea. The glasses are specially treated for hot beverages, but, just to be on the safe side, a silver spoon is often placed inside the glass to prevent it from cracking. There are special holders with handles for the glasses; some of these are made of silver. Sugar and lemon may be added to tea, but Russians often prefer to stir in a couple of large spoonfuls of strawberry jam or some other fruit preserve. Coffee is also popular.

Bread and Caviar

Russians eats lots of bread. They try to buy it while it's hot, just out of the oven. White bread is eaten on holidays or special occasions, although hard rolls, made of white flour, are used for hero-type sandwiches. Dark rye bread is the most popular bread. Supermarkets often sell a dark Russian-style rye or Jewish rye bread. Spread with butter and jam, or eaten with a slice of cheese or meat, it's a delicious and healthy snack.

Caviar is an appetizer, often used as a spread on crackers. It is very salty and not everyone likes the taste. Actually, caviar is fish eggs, or roe, from either salmon or sturgeon. It is an expensive delicacy. Another popular appetizer is herring. It may be smoked (something like

Caviar is a special treat in the Russian diet.

English kippers) or the herring fish fillets may be rolled and marinated in a tomato-oil mixture or a sour cream sauce.

Soups and Salads

Salads are popular and are often eaten at breakfast. The most common are shredded carrots and sliced radishes and cucumbers, drenched with lots of sour cream. Another salad is made with diced cooked carrots, beets, and potatoes, then mixed in oil, herbs, and vinegar, which gives the salad its name of vinaigrette. Lettuce and tomatoes are also popular.

There are many hearty soups, which often make up the main meal, with plenty of rye bread. There is a cabbage soup called *shchyee*. It's hard to pronounce but it's good to eat! (Here's a hint on how to handle that "shch" sound, which is a separate letter in the Russian alphabet. Say the words "mar*sh ch*air" rapidly; then practice repeating that "shch" sound.) *Shchyee* is usually made with pork stock. Sometimes sauerkraut is used instead of fresh cabbage.

Borscht comes in two flavors. One is a thick vegetable soup that includes cabbage. The other is a beet soup, served either hot or cold, with diced chives and cucumbers, sliced hard-boiled eggs, and always with a dab of sour cream.

Other hot soups include mushroom and barley, chicken broth with meat dumplings, and thick fish soup called *solyanka ribnaya*. Cold soups are popular, too. In addition to cold beet borscht, there are fruit soups and a cold meat soup cooked in kvass, a drink made from rye bread.

Hot Foods

The main dish will include meat or fish and vegetables. The selection of vegetables is not varied, but there are beets, carrots, tomatoes, peas, string beans, cabbage, and always potatoes.

Potatoes are not only boiled or mashed, but are also served as pancakes and as a "cake" called kugel. To make pancakes or kugel, potatoes are grated and mixed with some flour and an egg or two. Pieces of onion and bacon are added, then the mixture is fried or baked. The "cake" is cut into squares. Both potato pancakes and potato kugel are served with sour cream.

Potatoes are also made into dumplings and filled with cottage cheese or meat. A dough is made of mashed and freshly grated potatoes, filled, and boiled. Some of the dumplings are shaped like blimps (they're called "zeppelins" in Russian). Melted butter is poured over them, or they are served with sour cream. Russians don't worry too much about cholesterol.

The meat dish might be a "cutlet," which could be a veal or pork chop, or just a large hamburger patty. Shashlik are pieces of lamb or pork grilled on skewers like shish kebabs. There are spicy goulashes (stews) and peppery sausages. Beef Stroganoff is sautéed hamburger or cubes of beef, cooked in a sour cream sauce with mushrooms. It is served with either noodles or kasha (cooked buckwheat).

Chicken is served grilled or roasted. Chicken Kiev is a boneless chicken breast, stuffed with butter (or margarine) and cheese, dipped in flour and bread crumbs, and deep-fried.

A typical Russian feast

Be careful when you stick a fork into it, because the hot melted butter, or margarine, will spurt out.

There is a variety of fish. Sturgeon, carp, pike, catfish, perch, and halibut are popular.

Dessert

Piroshki, or fritters, are popular. So are very thin pancakes, called blini, filled with jam, then rolled like an enchilada and sprinkled with powdered sugar. There are fruit puddings called *kissel*, as well as fresh fruit (apples, cherries, pears, and peaches). And there is also ice cream, called *marozhinaya*.

8. School Daze

Forty million Russian students study in 127,000 schools and are taught by two million teachers.

Much of the former Soviet pattern of education is currently followed, with some exceptions. Students are no longer forced to wear a standard uniform to school and communism is no longer taught as a required subject. History books are being revised and books previously banned are now being read.

Classes are held six days a week. Summer vacation is limited to July and August, and there is a Christmas break. Most important is the fact that all lesson plans and curricula, including school textbooks, are adopted in Moscow for the entire country. There are no independent school districts; education in Russia is still uniform and centralized, but this pattern is being reviewed and may change.

An important official in Russian education described the system to a visiting American professor. "At this very hour, I think that in every fourth grade classroom, across this country, every youngster is studying geography, and he or she is probably on page 27 of the same textbook."

Cradle through Kindergarten

Babies may be admitted to nurseries as early as three months of age. Toddlers then move on to preschool and kindergarten activities, which begin at the age of three years. Elementary school doesn't begin until a child is six or seven years old. Parents may decide which school they prefer, providing there is room in the school for the child.

This type of early childhood education came about because most mothers had to work—along with the fathers—and child care was essential. Nurseries were usually located close to where the mothers worked. These mothers were given a paid leave of two months before the birth of a child, and at least two months after the child was born. This leave was extended if twins were born, or if the mother had medical complications in childbirth. A carryover from Soviet days is the policy that allows working mothers to stay at home with their children up to three years, without the danger of losing their jobs. They are paid half of their normal salary during this period, but do not lose any pension (simailar to social security) benefits.

The Educational Ladder

Education is required for nine grades. After the ninth grade, some students continue with vocational training. The brightest ninth graders stay on for another two years to prepare for the university or a professional institute.

Elementary grades are one through four. The "middle level" school is for grades five through nine. "Secondary" (or high school) education is for grades ten and eleven. There is no twelfth or "senior" year in the Russian system.

At the conclusion of the ninth grade, all students take an

A Russian kindergarten class

exam in language skills and mathematics. Those who do well are encouraged to continue in the general academic program. Those who do poorly in the exam are directed to the vocational or trade program.

Vocational training prepares a student to be a nurse's aide or an auto mechanic, for example. Those students who plan to go on to the university study history, mathematics, languages, and science. Every student must master at least one foreign language; English is the most popular.

It isn't easy to enter a university or scientific institute. There is lots of competition, and successful students must pass special examinations with a high grade. Most students spend an entire year preparing themselves for those exams. If they are successful, they will spend five years in the university and obtain a master's degree, or six years to acquire a medical degree.

There are some 500 universities and scientific institutes in Russia, but the most famous ones are in Moscow and St. Petersburg. Among these are the Moscow State University, the St. Petersburg Law Faculty, the School of Engineering, the Institute for International Relations, the Foreign Language Institute, the Institute for Foreign Trade, and the Institute of Dramatic Art.

Special Schools

Beginning with the second grade, students who qualify may apply to attend special schools that emphasize a particular field, such as music, mathematics, science, a sport, or a foreign language, in addition to the standard curriculum. In a school that specializes in English, for example, half of the courses are taught in English. Competition to enter such schools is intense. Very demanding exams must be passed to satisfy the strict entrance requirements.

Some Problems Students Face

Students in Russia do not have enough textbooks, and the ones they have are not up-to-date. The books are being rewritten to take out the propaganda and errors found in the old Soviet texts. In fact, final exams in history were cancelled in 1988 because no one was sure about the accuracy of what had been taught. Many teachers bring newspapers and magazines to class so that students can study geography and current events.

In the absence of books, much of the instruction comes from the teacher by way of a lecture or a recitation. The student is expected to take notes and memorize facts. Oral and written examinations are frequent. Teachers and students are beginning to learn how to have group discussions about various topics and differing points of view. A class recently discussed the topic of "betrayal" because, in the past, communists often encouraged children to report anticommunist activities of their neighbors and even their parents. In another class, discussing the works of Tolstoy, the teacher asked, "Where does the feeling of happiness come from?" The class decided the answer was "When one is in harmony with the world."

Most classrooms are attractive, with desks, chairs or benches, bookcases, and chalkboards. There may be flowers to decorate the teacher's desk. However, there is a shortage of computers, photocopying machines, and laboratory equipment. Under the Soviet regime, only persons with security clearance could use computers and copiers.

Many of the school buildings are old and need to be repaired, especially in smaller towns. A 1992 survey shows that a third of Russian schools have no running water and that 40 percent have no indoor toilets. Some do not have central heating. Some of the rural schools have dormitories, and students return to their homes only on weekends.

Despite the problems and shortages, education is taken very seriously in Russia. Lots of homework is assigned. There is much emphasis on history, science, and mathematics. In fact, the basic concepts of algebra are taught as early as the first grade.

Russians are proud of their culture and heritage. In the Soviet era, education was seen mostly as a means to strengthen the political system; students studied to become "useful" to the state. Education in Russia is no longer political and is seen to have value in and of itself. Excellence is emphasized.

Students are expected to clean their classrooms and school corridors. Each spring they help their parents and neighbors tidy up the parks. Young men in the university spend one day each week in military training.

Education is free, even in the universities. In fact, students in higher educational institutions receive a monthly allowance to pay for their room and board. The government, in return, asks the students to repay this amount through community service after they have graduated.

What about grades? Students begin to receive grades in the third grade. The grading system uses numbers from two to five. Five is best; two is unsatisfactory. These grades are often called out loud by the teacher, so everyone in the class knows what each person has received.

Beyond Classwork

Religion is taught in Russian schools but is a voluntary program. The teaching of religion was forbidden during the days of communism. Until a student is 14 years old, parents decide whether the student will take such classes; after age 14, the student decides.

Two generations of Russians

Youth organizations such as Komsomol, the Young Communist League, have disappeared in the schools. During the Soviet era, it was practically impossible to enter a university without first being a member of this organization; this is no longer the case. However, groups such as the Young Pioneers have continued. There are many similarities to Western Scouting programs. Young Pioneers have after-school clubs and operate summer camps.

Seven major magazines are published for young readers. Among these are *Koster* (*Campfire*) and *Yuny Naturalist* (*The Young Naturalist*).

School-sponsored sports programs are popular, as we will see in the next chapter. Glee clubs, bands, and drama groups are usually community activities, and are not sponsored by the school.

Many schools are open 12 hours a day, although regular classes are held for only half of this time. You might think of the typical Russian school as a combination of a regular school, a community youth center, a Scout program, a YMCA or YWCA, and an after-school tutoring or athletic program.

9. Russians Love Sports

One out of four Russians participates in some kind of sport. This might be soccer, swimming, ice-skating, cycling, or a dozen other physical activities. Baseball has been introduced and golf courses have been built in Moscow and St. Petersburg. Rifle marksmanship and parachute jumping are also considered sports.

Sports "palaces" were built in all major cities during the Soviet era. Most of these have been converted into giant health clubs where members keep their bodies in top condition.

Physical fitness begins in the first grade of school. Six-year-olds have daily workouts through simple exercises and gymnastics. When a child turns 11, and shows a special aptitude for a sport, he or she is encouraged to transfer to a "sports school." Regular classes continue and the student must maintain high grades to stay in the program. However, special classes in sports are held in the afternoons.

Not every sport is available in every school. Instead, "clusters" of sports are offered. For example, one school might combine track, wrestling, and hockey. Another would specialize in swimming, acrobatic gymnastics, and volleyball. Basketball and soccer are always popular.

The Olympics

The former Soviet Union fostered sports programs and gave scholarships to promising youths, and Russia still supports its

Moscow circus acrobats

athletes. Russian athletes now perform as the Unified Team representing the Commonwealth of Independent States.

   Although the USSR did not participate in the Olympics until 1952, its athletes soon showed their skill in world competition. Through 1992 former Soviet and Unified Team athletes had won a total of 88 gold medals, 63 silver medals, and 67 bronze medals in the Olympic Winter Games; and they had won 441 gold, 361 silver, and 318 bronze medals in the Summer Games.

   At the 1992 Winter Olympics at Albertville, France, the

Unified Team took second place with 9 gold medals, 6 silver, and 8 bronze medals. At Barcelona, Spain, in the Summer Games held in 1992, the Unified Team placed first with 45 gold medals, 38 silver, and 29 bronze.

The 1980 Summer Olympics, held in Moscow, were boycotted by 62 nations, including the United States, as a protest against the Soviet invasion of Afghanistan. In reprisal the Soviet Union, joined by 14 other nations, boycotted the 1984 Summer Olympics in Los Angeles. The former USSR rejoined the international sports event for the Summer Games in Seoul, South Korea, in 1988.

Champions

Women gymnasts have been consistent medal-winners. Many adults will remember tiny Olga Korbut from Belarus, who charmed the world in 1972 with her daring skill on the bars and vault. Tatiana Lisenko starred on the balance beam in Barcelona in 1992.

Russian women have set more track records than Russian men. Russian men excel in such events as the hammer throw and the pole vault and are consistently skillful in gymnastics, weightlifting, and wrestling. Alexander Medved is a champion wrestler.

Russian athletes are especially good in winter sports such as speed skating and figure skating, luge, cross-country skiing, and ice hockey. The Soviet hockey team won Olympic gold medals in 1956, 1968, 1972, 1984, and 1988. It was considered a major upset when the U.S.

hockey team beat the Soviet champions at Lake Placid, New York, in 1980.

Team Sports

Many of the popular team sports played in Russia have come from other countries. Soccer, which originated in England, is Russia's number one team sport. There are more than a hundred thousand soccer fields, and every large city has its own professional team. Outside the United States, soccer is called football. That seems accurate because only the feet (and sometimes the head) are used to move the ball.

There is growing interest in American-style football, which is seen occasionally on television. Hockey was first played in Canada and this fast-paced and usually low-scoring game is well liked and much played in Russia. Basketball is taught and played in Russian schools. Soviet teams won the Olympic gold medal in 1972 and 1988.

Volleyball is another American invention, which is now an Olympic event. In Russia it is played by boys and girls. American-style baseball was introduced in Russia by students from Cuba. Russian children have long played a game called *lapta*, which is a close cousin to baseball.

Russian boys play a miniversion of soccer, on a smaller field, as well as a kind of wrestling and judo called sambo. Soccer players have "leather ball" clubs; hockey players, "golden puck" clubs. Russian children build "auto-scooter" racers, which are similar to soapbox derby vehicles.

News about major sports events is reported on the front

A friendly U.S.-Russian hockey game!

pages of Russian newspapers. Olympic Games were tele-
vised throughout Russia in all 11 time zones. Russians are
both sports participants and eager fans.

Mental Gymnastics

Russians consider chess to be a sport because it exercises the
brain. You see it played everywhere: on trains, on park
benches, and, of course, in tournaments. The communist
leader Vladimir Lenin was said to have played a game of
chess every day of his life.

Chess is a very old game that came to Europe by way
of India and Persia in the sixth century. Chess is played on
a checkerboard. It is a military strategy game played with
castles, knights, bishops, pawns (foot soldiers), and a queen
and king. The name for chess in Russian is *shakh-maht*,
which sounds a bit like "checkmate." *Check* or *shakh* may
have come from the Persian (or Iranian) word shah, which
means "king."

International chess competition began in 1851. Alexander Alekhine was the first Russian to win the world chess
championship, a title he held from 1927 to 1935. Mikhail
Botvinnik held three world titles, from 1948 to 1956, 1958 to
1960, and 1961 to 1963. He was succeeded by the Russian
Tigran Petrosian, who held the title from 1963 to 1969.
Bobby Fischer, an American, defeated Boris Spassky, a
Russian who held the title from 1969 to 1972. Fischer lost
his title to Anatoly Karpov in 1975. International chess was
dominated thereafter by two Russians: Anatoly Karpov

and Gary Kasparov, who were rivals for many years. Their most recent tournament of 24 games, played in France in 1990, was won by Kasparov, for which he received $1.7 million. (Bobby Fischer came out of retirement in 1992 to challenge his old rival Boris Spassky, now a French citizen. They played 30 games, with Fischer winning 10 to 5; the other games were "draws." Spassky has since again been defeated by Judit Polgar, a 16-year-old Hungarian girl who is already a grand master.)

Instruction in chess for Russian children begins in kindergarten, but gets very serious in the fifth grade, when students learn the plays (or "gambits") of the famous champions. Boys and girls both play and enjoy chess.

The highest rank in chess is grand master, for winners of major tournaments. A master is qualified to play in restricted competition. Ranking is determined by the International Chess Federation. Four thousand Russian children have achieved the rank of master!

10. Russians in America

Each time you look at a Lincoln penny, you see a reminder of a Russian immigrant to the United States. His name was Victor David Brenner and he was a sculptor. He was born in 1871 in Lithuania, which was then a part of the Russian empire. He came to the United States in 1890. In 1909 he was asked to design a coin that would celebrate the 100th birthday of Abraham Lincoln. This was the first American coin to honor a single individual. Although slightly modified in 1959, the Lincoln penny remains very much as Mr. Brenner designed it.

The most recent U.S. Census (1990) shows that since 1820, when census records were begun, more than 3.5 million people from Russia and the former Soviet Union have emigrated to the United States. It is estimated that there are some 50,000 people of Russian descent in Canada.

Slavic and Baltic immigrants arrived much earlier than Victor Brenner. A Ukrainian, Lavrenty (Lawrence) Bohun, was one of the 105 settlers at Jamestown in 1607, but little is known about him or how he came to join the English settlers.

The first actual emigrant from Russia to the British colonies in North America was Charles Thiel. He was born to German parents in St. Petersburg and was trained in medicine and pharmacy. Somehow he displeased the empress

Catherine the Great and fled to the New World. He settled in Philadelphia in 1769, seven years before the colonies declared their independence. He changed his last name to Cist, and changed his profession as well. First, he became a printer and a publisher. One of the books he published was Thomas Paine's pamphlet "The American Crisis." Later, Charles Cist discovered anthracite, an extremely hard and long-burning coal. He founded the Lehigh Coal Mining Company in Pennsylvania.

Many Russians came to work in those coal mines. There is a city in Pennsylvania named for one of them. It's called Gallitzin, and is located near Altoona. The city is named for Demetrius Augustine Gallitzin, who had been a prince and, of course, a member of the royal family. He left his Russian Orthodox church to become a Roman Catholic priest and missionary. He gave up both his royal title and fortune to help farmers and Indians in the Allegheny Mountains.

A Russian Colony in North America

Russia once owned the land that is now Alaska. Russian settlers in 1799 established a village called New Archangel, now called Sitka. Russians built other outposts for their growing fur-trading business. In fact, to protect that business, Russia built two forts in what today is northern California. The United States purchased Alaska from Russia in 1867, paying $7 million, or about two cents for each acre.

A fascinating immigrant-settler from those Russian

colonial days was Ivan Veniaminov. He was a missionary who came to Alaska with his family. He learned the Indian Aleut language and compiled the first dictionary and grammar in Aleut. He also translated parts of the Bible. He was named Alaska's first bishop and established 36 churches during his ten-year stay. He built St. Michael's Cathedral, in Sitka, which is still standing. When he returned to Russia, he was appointed the metropolitan of Moscow, which is the highest post in the Russian Orthodox church.

The Immigrants

Although Russian peasant-serfs were given their freedom in 1861, it would be many years before they saved enough money to move to new homes in new lands.

The first Russians who came to North America were rich people such as Charles Thiel and Father Gallitzin. Many of them had close ties with the royal court. Many of them had wanted to reform the monarchy. Some were radical revolutionaries.

Vladimir Stolishnikoff was one of those radicals. He escaped arrest in Russia and was able to come to the United States. He was an architect and later helped design New York City's famous Carnegie Hall.

Another wealthy refugee was Peter Dementev (a name he changed to Demens). He was an engineer and he built a railroad in Florida. He also laid out a new city in Florida, calling it St. Petersburg, after his birthplace in Russia.

By the early 1900s, many peasant farmers, most of them

The Russian influence is seen in Alaska.

children of former serfs, began to come to America. Somehow they had saved the $50 it took to pay for passage to cross the Atlantic Ocean. Many Jewish families also emigrated from Russia during this period.

For these farmers and workers, life had become unbearable in Russia. Industrial workers labored 12 hours a day in factories that were not safe. Farmers had very little land but many debts. The Jews were harassed and persecuted, forced to live in ghettos or restricted areas. Although Russia did have a constitution, the common people felt they had no rights and no future. As the 20th century began, and war seemed likely with Japan, many Russians decided not to fight for the czar but to seek their fortune elsewhere.

Russian immigrants did not always find fortune in America. Since they did not speak English, the only jobs they could find were in coal mines, steel mills, or stockyards. A few of the luckier immigrants found work on farms. Some of them acquired "homesteads" in Canada. There, if you were willing to clear the land, build a shelter, begin to farm, and live on your land for seven years, the government gave you 360 acres as a homestead.

Life became difficult for many Russians during World War I (1914–1918). They faced suspicion and discrimination from their neighbors. Russians did not mingle with other Americans, but kept to themselves in their own communities, speaking their native language. Some of them became active in labor unions. A few of them were communists. After the communists in Russia gained control and made a separate peace with Germany, Americans, who were still at war with Germany, looked on the Russian immigrants as traitors.

Religious Refugees

Many Russians came to North America to find religious freedom. Some were descendants of German Mennonites who had left Holland and Germany for Ukraine, at the invitation of Catherine the Great. Mennonites were pacifists, believing that it was wrong for them to fight in a war, no matter what the circumstances might be. The empress Catherine understood their position and allowed them to live their peaceful lives, knowing that they were hardworking and capable farmers. However, after her death, other czars stressed Russian nationalism and military power. It was no longer safe to be both a German and a pacifist, and these Mennonites, who were now Russian citizens, began to look for a new home in the Americas. They settled in Pennsylvania, Indiana, Kansas, and western Canada. Other Germans living in Russia, who were Catholics or Lutherans, emigrated to the Dakotas.

Members of another Russian immigrant group settled near Los Angeles and were called Molokans. Molokan is a nickname, in Russian, for "milk drinkers." The Molokans are a religious sect that split off from the Russian Orthodox church. They drink only milk during Lent, the 40-day period before Easter. Like the Mennonites, they also refused to serve in the armed forces.

The Dukhobors, who settled in Canada, are similar to the

Molokans. They rejected the Russian Orthodox church, do not have priests, and are vegetarians. They were severely harassed in Russia and had to find a new country in which to live, if they were to survive. Their name is also a nickname, derived from the Russian word *dukh*, which means "spirit." Literally, their name means "spirit wrestler."

Russian Jews began their journeys to the New World in the late 1880s. Many Jews had been killed or crippled in the pogroms, a Russian word that means devastation. Their homes and farms had been burned. Russian Jews were restricted to an area called the Pale of Settlement. They were forbidden to travel "beyond the Pale," whose limits extended from the Polish border to the Dnieper River, and from the Baltic to the Black Sea. The Jews emigrated because even living within this restricted area did not guarantee them physical safety.

After World War II

A new wave of immigrants came to North America following World War II (1939–1945). During that war, thousands of Soviet citizens were captured by the Nazis and sent to Germany as slave labor. Soviet Jews were victims of the Holocaust and were sent to extermination camps.

Following the war, many Russian survivors decided to remain in the West and not return to their homes. They were called DPs, or displaced persons. Thousands were granted new homes in the United States and Canada.

It was very difficult for Russian citizens to emigrate until the administration of Mikhail Gorbachev. His policy of perestroika allowed the "prisoners of conscience" and other dissidents to seek new homes in other countries, if they so chose.

Famous Citizens

The Western world has been greatly enriched by these talented people. Let's review some of their names.

Vladimir Zworkykin is called the "father of television." He invented the iconoscope, the camera tube that makes television possible. Igor Sikorsky was an aviation pioneer, best known as the inventor and designer of helicopters. George Gamov was an atomic scientist who worked on the theory of nuclear fission. A crater on the moon has been named for him. Selman Waksman discovered streptomycin, an antibiotic.

Among writers who have adopted the West are Vladimir Nabokov and Sholom Aleichem (real name: Solomon Rabinowitz). Aleichem wrote about Jewish life in Russia and one of his stories is the basis for the musical (and motion picture) *Fiddler on the Roof.* Other writers include Nobel Prize winner Alexander Solzhenitsyn, Joseph Brodsky, and Dr. Isaac Asimov. Asimov wrote more than 100 books but may be best known for his science fiction.

Many famous musicians have come to our shores. Igor Stravinsky and Dmitri Shostakovich, composers. Dmitri's father, Maxim, conductor. Sergei Rachmaninov and Vladimir Horowitz, pianists. Jascha Heifetz and Isaac Stern, violinists. Serge Koussevitsky, former conductor of the Boston Symphony. Dmitri Tiomkin, the frequent Academy Award winner for his movie scores. Sol Hurok, a promotor of concerts, was a Russian-American. So was the songwriter Irving Berlin, who wrote what many people consider a second national anthem, "God Bless America."

Among our newest musicians is Mstislav Rostropovich, a cellist and conductor of the National Symphony in Washington, D.C. His wife, Galina Vishnevskaya, is a well-known soprano and opera star. Rostropovich won the Lenin Prize for music in 1964 but was ordered to leave the Soviet Union because he publicly defended such political dissidents as Andrei Sakharov. He returned to his native land in 1990 with the National Symphony and was given back his Russian citizenship. In the closing concert of the tour, in Moscow, Rostropovich paid tribute to his adopted land, the United States, by leading the National Symphony in Sousa's "The Stars and Stripes Forever."

Russians have contributed much to American ballet. George Balanchine founded the New York City Ballet and was one of the great choreographers of modern times. His parents were Georgian but he was born in St. Petersburg; the family name was Balanchivadze. Other famous Russian ballet performers who emigrated to the United States were Mikhail Baryshnikov, Alexander Godunov, and Natalia Makarova.

Many actors have Eastern European origins. Akim Tamiroff, who played dozens of character roles in motion pictures, was born in Baku, Russia. The parents of several

The noted Russian dancer Mikhail Baryshnikov

Hollywood stars came from Russia: Natalie Wood was born Natasha Gurdin; Kirk Douglas was born Issur Danielovich Demsky; Mike Nichols was born Mikhail Igor Peschkovsky.

Family Ties

Russians fondly remember their motherland. Many older people prefer to speak and argue in Russian, to practice their Orthodox faith, and to read newspapers and books in their own language and Cyrillic script. Many have fought homesickness for more than half a century, and some are just now feeling free to visit their birthplace for one last time.

The children and grandchildren of Russian immigrants are thoroughly American and Canadian. Remembering their immigrant heritage, they treasure the Old World but are busy helping to create the New.

11. What about the Future?

Russia is living through a transition from an economy that was run entirely by the government in Moscow to one that permits individuals to run their own businesses or farms or factories. To put it another way, Russia is moving from communism to capitalism. Russia is also moving from totalitarianism (total control by a single political party) to democracy (with freedom of speech and activity, with many political parties).

Although the Communist party has lost its official power, it has not disappeared. At one time, it had 20 million members throughout the Soviet Union. It is estimated that 5 million of these—including Boris Yeltsin—resigned from the party. This still leaves many communists who are members of the Congress or who are managers of industries and who might like to return to the old ways.

Russia faces many problems. Its currency, the ruble, has lost its value, prices are constantly increasing, and wages do not keep up with inflation. Many people are without work as older, inefficient factories are closed. Many people are homeless. The soldiers of the former Soviet Union who are returning from Hungary, Poland, Czechoslovakia, East Germany, and the Baltic republics cannot find places to live. Food and fuel are in short supply.

The SALT (Strategic Arms Limitation Talks) and START (Strategic Arms Reduction Talks) agreements have

A Russian reader keeps up with the news.

reduced the threat of nuclear war between the former Soviet Union and the United States. The first START treaty was signed by Presidents George Bush and Mikhail Gorbachev in Moscow just before the attempted overthrow of Gorbachev's government. That treaty contains 700 pages that describe the proposed cuts and the rules for disarming nuclear weapons. A second START treaty was signed in early 1993 by Bush and Yeltsin.

However, not all nuclear weapons will be destroyed by either side. A large worry for everyone is the fact that nuclear weapons of the former Soviet Union are located in four countries: Russia, Ukraine, Belarus, and Kazakhstan. There is need for much more negotiation and many new agreements among these countries themselves, as well as with other nuclear powers. The START treaty must be ratified by each country's legislature before it takes effect.

There are other problems that are concerned with defense. Who is responsible for the navy, for example, particularly in the Black Sea? Russia and Ukraine are debating this question. Ukraine has yet to sign many CIS agreements. Will there be a unified army, or will each republic have its own? Will the generals and admirals remain loyal to the new Commonwealth? How will they cope with their personal loss of prestige as part of what is now a vanished superpower?

And what will happen to the former secret police, the dreaded KGB? In Russia it has been split into two organizations: the Ministry of Security and the Russian Foreign Intelligence Service. Radio Free Europe reports that these two security organizations have nearly 140,000 officers and agents, many of whom served the former Soviet Union, which suggests that the old KGB is still alive and well.

Other issues that trouble the Commonwealth relate to its many different nationalities. More than 100 languages are spoken in the former Soviet Union, 50 of them in Russia alone. Many of the larger ethnic groups would like to govern themselves in their own individual states. Some of these who seek independence are Abhazia, Checheno-Ingush, Nagorno-Karabakh, and Tatarstan. Fighting has occurred in Tajikistan, Armenia, Azerbaijan, and Moldava.

Another major problem, which may take years to solve, is how to correct the damage done to Russia's environment. Because the Soviet government had no written laws to protect the ecology, major rivers and lakes have been polluted by

Moscow's Red Square

industrial chemicals. Nine nuclear power plants still operate within Russia. They are similar to the one at Chernobyl, Ukraine, which had a meltdown in 1986. Radioactive waste has been dumped in the Arctic north in the Kara Sea and the Barents Sea off the island of Novaya Zemlya. Similar dumping has taken place in the sea of Okhotsk, which flows into the Pacific.

Throughout Russia's long history, there have been czars and dictators who governed with an iron and cruel hand. But

Russia has also had many kings and leaders who tried gradually to give the Russian people more freedom and more opportunities. Despite all their problems, the Russian people today have the means to achieve more independence than ever before. Most Russians believe there can be no turning back to the old ways of tyranny and fear. They look forward to a new constitution and new democratic leadership.

A *new* Russia has, indeed, been born. But as is the case with any newborn baby, Russia must crawl before it can walk. Newspapers and magazines will report its stumbles. The rest of the world hopes that Russia will mature steadily and safely into a productive and prosperous democracy.

Appendix

Embassies and Consulates of the Russian Federation in the United States and Canada

Embassy of the Russian Federation
1125 16th Street, NW
Washington, DC 20036

Tel: (202) 628-7551 and 8548

Permanent Mission of the Russian Federation
in the United Nations
136 East 67th Street
New York, NY 10021

Tel: (212) 861-4900

Embassy of the Russian Federation
52 Range Road
Ottawa, ON K1N 8JB

Tel: (613) 236-7220

Glossary

blini (BLEE-nee)—pancakes

borscht (BORSHT)—soup, made either from beets, or from meat and vegetables

boyar (bow-YAHR)—Russian count or nobleman

commissar (KOH-mee-sahr)—a local political leader

cosmonaut (KAUZ-mo-not)—Soviet astronaut

czar (ZAHR)—king or emperor; sometimes spelled "tsar"

dacha (DAH-chah)—a country or vacation home

dukh (DOOKH)—spirit or soul

duma (DOO-mah)—the first Russian congress

glasnost (GLAHS-nost)—openness, freedom of speech

goulash (GOO-lahsh)—a meat stew

grozny (GRAWZ-nee)—to be feared or dreaded; a name for Czar Ivan IV, known as Ivan the Terrible

icon (EYE-kon)—a sacred painting in the Russian Orthodox church

izba (IZ-bah)—farmhouse or log cabin

kasha (KAH-sha)—cooked buckwheat

kissel (KEE-sell)—fruit pudding

kistka (KEES-ta)—a small writing instrument used to scratch designs onto the waxy surface of a *pysanky*

kolkhoz (kol-HOZ)—collective farms

kopek (KOH-pek)—smallest unit of Russian money, like a penny

koulich (KOO-lich)—a special cake baked at Eastertime

krasnaya (KRAHS-nah-yah)—a word that means either "red" or "beautiful"

kugel (KOO-gel)—a potato cake

kulak (KOO-lahk)—farm owners

kvass (kuh-VAS)—a drink made from sour rye bread

lapta (LAHP-ta)—a game similar to baseball

marozhinaya (mah-RAW-zhin-ah-ya)—ice cream

muzhiki (moo-ZHEE-kee)—peasants, farm workers

perestroika (perry-STROY-ka)—restructure, reforming

piroshki (pee-ROSH-kee)—fritters

pogrom (po-GROHM)—a violent attack upon Jews

pysanky (pih-SAHN-key)—decorated Easter eggs

rodina (raw-DEE-nah)—Russian term for "motherland" or "beloved country"

ruble (ROO-bul)—basic unit of money, like the dollar

sambo (SAHM-bow)—a sport combining elements of judo and wrestling

samovar (sahm-oh-VAHR)—appliance used to make tea

shakh-maht (shak-MAHT)—chess

shashlik (SHASH-lik)—grilled meat (often lamb) on a skewer

shchyee (SHCH-yee)—cabbage soup

solyanka ribnaya (sohl-YAHN-kah REEB-nah-yah)—fish soup

sovkhoz (sov-KOZ)—state-owned farms

steppe (STEP)—plain or prairie

taiga (TAI-gah)—a birch-and-pine forest

zemstvo (ZEHMS-tvoh)—local council or board of nobles, townspeople, and farmer peasants

Selected Bibliography

Clark, James I. *The Soviet Union* (People and Culture series). Evanston, Ill.: McDougal, Littell & Co., 1989.

Eubank, Nancy. *The Russians in America*. Minneapolis: Lerner Publications, 1973.

Gorbachev, Mikhail S. *Perestroika: New Thinking for Our Country and the World*. New York: Harper & Row, 1987.

Gwertzman, Bernard, and Michael T. Kaufman, eds. *The Decline and Fall of the Soviet Empire*. New York: Times Books, 1992.

Kennan, George F. *Russia and the West Under Lenin and Stalin*. Boston: Little, Brown, 1961.

Kublin, Michael and Hyman. *Russia*. Boston: Houghton Mifflin, 1990.

Lawrence, Sir John. *A History of Russia* (6th edition). New York: New American Library, 1978.

Maddox, Robert J. *The Unknown War with Russia*. San Rafael, Calif.: Presidio Press, 1977.

Magocsi, Paul R. *The Russian Americans*. New York: Chelsea House, 1989.

Morton, Miriam. *The Making of Champions: Soviet Sports for Children and Teenagers*. New York: Atheneum, 1974.

Shipler, David K. *Russia: Broken Idols, Solemn Dreams*. New York: Times Books, 1983.

Smith, Hedrick. *The New Russians*. New York: Random House, 1990.

Wilson, Andrew, and Nina Bachkator. *Russia and the Commonwealth: A to Z*. New York: HarperCollins, 1992.

Index

About the Author

John Gillies is well acquainted with Eastern Europe. As a young man in the late 1930s, he lived in Lithuania, where his father had been born and raised before coming to the United States. He has since visited the former Soviet Union twice in the 1980s, and has returned to Lithuania annually since 1991. Through facts, honesty, and humor, Mr. Gillies hopes that an understanding and appreciation of the new Russia will be achieved.

The author has worked in many fields. He has been a radio and television announcer, an actor, a missionary, and a communications consultant. His published works include a play and ten books, including *Señor Alcalde: A Biography of Henry Cisneros*, also published by Dillon Press. Mr. Gillies also wrote Dillon's Discovering Our Heritage title, *The Soviet Union*. This is a revised and updated version of that book.

Mr. Gillies and his wife, Carolyn, live in Austin, Texas. They have three children, four grandchildren, and a Scottie named Cullen.